THE NEANDERTHALS

The Neanderthal is among the most mysterious relatives of *Homo sapiens*: Was he a dull, club-swinging muscleman, or a being with developed social behavior and the ability to speak, to plan precisely, and even to develop views on the afterlife?

For many, the Neanderthals are an example of primitive humans, but new discoveries suggest that this image needs to be revised. One hundred thousand years ago in ice-age Europe, there emerged people who managed to cope well with the difficult climate—Neanderthals. They formed an organized society, hunted mammoths, and could make fire. They were able to pass on knowledge, caring for the old and the disabled, burying their dead, and placing gifts on their graves. Yet they became extinct, despite their cultural abilities.

This richly illustrated book, written for general audiences, provides a competent look at the history, living conditions, and culture of the Neanderthal.

Friedemann Schrenk is Professor of Vertebrate Palaeobiology at Johann Wolfgang Goethe University, Frankfurt, Germany, and Head of the Palaeoanthropological Department at the Senckenberg Research Institute in Frankfurt.

Stephanie Müller is a science writer and editor in the Section of Public Understanding at the Senckenberg Research Institute.

PEOPLES OF THE ANCIENT WORLD

This series stands as the first port of call for anyone who wants to know more about the historically important peoples of the ancient world and the early middle ages.

Reliable, up-to-date and with special attention paid to the peoples' enduring legacy and influence, *Peoples of the Ancient World* will ensure the continuing prominence of these crucial figures in modern-day study and research.

THE NEANDERTHALS

*Friedemann Schrenk and
Stephanie Müller,
in collaboration with
Christine Hemm*

Translated by Phyllis G. Jestice

Die Neandertaler (by Friedemann Schrenk,
Stephanie Müller, in collaboration with
Christine Hemm)

Routledge
Taylor & Francis Group

LONDON AND NEW YORK

First published in 2005 by
Verlag C.H. Beck

English translation, translated by
Phyllis G. Jestice, published in 2009
by Routledge
2 Park Square, Milton Park, Abingdon, Oxon OX14 4RN

Simultaneously published in the USA and Canada
by Routledge
270 Madison Ave., New York, NY 100016

Routledge is an imprint of the Taylor & Francis Group, an informa business

© Verlag C.H. Beck oHG, München 2005

Typeset in Times New Roman by
Keystroke, 28 High Street, Tettenhall, Wolverhampton
Printed and bound in Great Britain by
TJ International Ltd, Padstow, Cornwall

British Library Cataloguing in Publication Data
A catalogue record for this book is available from the British Library

Library of Congress Cataloging in Publication Data
Schrenk, Friedemann.
[Neanderthaler. English]
The Neanderthals/by Friedemann Schrenk and Stephanie Müller; in
collaboration with Christine Hemm; translated by Phyllis G. Jestice.
    p. cm. – (Peoples of the ancient world)
    1. Neanderthals. I. Müller, Stephanie. II. Hemm, Christine. III. Title.
GN285.S58 2008
569.9′86–dc22   2008016079

ISBN10: 0–415–42519–0 (hbk)
ISBN10: 0–415–42520–4 (pbk)
ISBN10: 0–203–88966–5 (ebk)

ISBN13: 978–0–415–42519–3 (hbk)
ISBN13: 978–0–415–42520–9 (pbk)
ISBN13: 978–0–203–88966–4 (ebk)

CONTENTS

CONTENTS

FIGURES

FOREWORD

This work about the Neanderthals is one of many books on the market that deal with our early ancestors. Granted, this book has nothing revolutionary to say on the subject of what we know about this archaic human variety, nor how that knowledge has been received in the scientific and popular communities. Nonetheless, a volume in this format—brief and fact-based, but still comprehensible—makes a contribution by providing a comprehensive overview of the history of the Neanderthals, their relatives, their habitat, and the century and a half of research about them. The 150th anniversary of the first publicized Neanderthal find, made in Germany in 1856, merely offers a convenient occasion for this book.

During our investigation of African pre-hominids and primitive humans, considering their significance to the regional historical consciousness of modern people, we discovered astonishing parallels in the history of the science of paleoanthropology (the branch of research dedicated to the history of our forebears) in both Africa and Europe. This can be seen, first, in modern paleoanthropology's ever greater tendency to regard not just morphology (the study of the form of a find) and its geological age but also its geographical location. The biogeography of fossils is an essential precondition to creating a scientific interpretation that also takes changes in habitat into account. This applies to the reconstruction of the early hominids of Africa just as much as it does to the Neanderthals and their contemporaries. The recognition of regional developments in human prehistory provides, so to speak, a series of signposts that can lead to a detailed picture of human evolution. Climatic shift and the changes it produces in habitats and in the availability of food provides a second factor in the evolution of our ancestors, one that is equally significant for research. Whereas 2.5 million years ago, thanks to extreme changes, cultural evolution had its starting point—with the "invention" of stone tools—the Neanderthals were the first humans to settle in the inhospitable regions of ice-age Europe. There they devised and used tool techniques that made it possible for them to survive—for a considerable length of time. Third, we consider public opinion, the history of how these finds were received. European public consciousness was for a long time marked by a low regard for the Neanderthals. They were spoken of as stupid brutes, as animal-like beasts that, armed with a jawbone, lurked behind rocky outcroppings. In Africa too, up to the present time there has been little awareness of or public interest in the historical significance of their own African origins. Scholarship, as an intermediary between scientific research and the public, thus has an obligation to spread our state of knowledge about the heritage of human history in a form suited to general audiences. Scholarship should create knowledge, in Europe as in Africa. Thus it was also delightful for us to approach the Neanderthals with a certain scientific-geographical distance and curiosity, for the creation of this book also sprang from a desire to present to the public the significance of the continents in human evolution, and to make us conscious of the many-sided interdependence that, since the beginning of the human condition, has been a hallmark of our species. It is a forceful argument for acceptance and tolerance between humans, whether they be in fossil form or alive today, and whether they come from Africa, Europe, or some other part of the earth.

Stephanie Müller, Friedmann Schrenk
Frankfurt am Main, May 2005

1

THE HISTORY OF THE NEANDERTHAL

DISCOVERY

Mettmann, 4. September. In the neighboring Neander Valley, the so-called "Rocks," a surprising discovery was made in recent days. During the breaking away of the limestone cliffs, which cannot be sufficiently lamented from the point of view of aesthetics, a cave was uncovered, which over the course of centuries had been filled with clay sediment. Upon digging out this clay, a human rib was found, which doubtless would have been unregarded and lost had not, fortunately, Dr. Fuhlrott of Elberfeld secured and investigated the find.

Site of find, fossil, and finder. This contemporary account of the discovery of the Neanderthal, later to be world famous, appeared in the Elberfeld newspaper on 6 September 1856. It seems rather paltry from a modern perspective. The first find of human fossils to be recognized as such was made in an era of technological and scientific upheaval. The Industrial Revolution had made its mark on Europe and the idea of evolution had already appeared. In 1758, a century before the find in the Neander Valley near Mettmann, the Swedish Christian and natural scientist Carl von Linné had classified human beings together with prosimians, monkeys, and bats in his hierarchy of mammal primates or "ruling animals." His contemporaries were indignant. After all, ever since the Middle Ages the ape had been viewed as a devil-created mockery of humanity. So to place the human being, created in the image of God, on a line with apes bordered on blasphemy. A hundred years later, in 1858, Charles Darwin threw open the question of human evolution with a single remark in his *Origin of Species*: "Light will be thrown on the origin of man and his history." A heretical sentence, which the first German translator of the work found so offensive that he did not translate it. Darwin's hidden thesis (and that of his often-forgotten fellow fighter Alfred Russel Wallace) that humans,

1

like all other living things, must be the result of an evolutionary process and not a unique divine act of creation, was revolutionary. Darwin himself first summed up his views on human origins in 1871 in his *Descent of Man*. In Germany, the zoologists Carl Vogt and Ernst Haeckel paved the way for the theory of evolution in scholarly circles. In 1863, Haeckel delivered a lecture in which he argued that there must have been a link, now extinct, between apes and humans. He named this "missing link" *Pithecanthropus alalus*—"non-speaking ape-man"—and foretold that the fossil remains of this ancestor would be found in southeast Asia. Haeckel's prophecy about the place of discovery would be fulfilled.

The origin of humanity has never been discussed with complete objectivity, since of course it is an issue that touches all human beings and is closely linked to ideological and political interests. Many regarded the extension of the human family tree into the animal kingdom as scandalous. As the bishop of Worcester's wife is supposed to have said after a conversation with Darwin's supporter Thomas Henry Huxley in 1860: "My dear, descended from the apes! Let us hope it is not true, but if it is, let us pray it will not become generally known." Neither the fervent hope of the pious bishop's wife nor the 1812 pronouncement of the French natural philosopher Georges, Baron de Cuvier, that "fossil man does not exist" kept fossil humans from winning recognition. The Neanderthal discovered in 1856 provided the first "living" evidence.

The Neander Valley near Mettmann, the discovery site of the first fossil evidence of primordial humans, was named after the Bremen theologian and hymnographer Joachim Neumann (composer of "Praise to the Lord, the Almighty, the King of Creation"). As was fashionable in 1670, he used the Greek translation of his name, "Neander" (Newman), in compliment to antiquity. Joachim Neander, at that time rector of the Düsseldorf Latin School, visited the "Rocks," as the area was called then, seeking inspiration from the mountains, crags, streams, and cliffs "with a special amazement." Whole generations of painters from the Düsseldorf Academy did the same. The Neander Valley became a locale for seeking the muses, a place of lyric poetry, sketches, and watercolors. It was doubtless the picturesque limestone cliffs and mysterious caves along the course of the Düssel River that enticed artists and town-dwellers to the "Rocks" (also called "Dog's Crag" locally), only two hours distant by coach. Countless excursion groups sent couriers to the nearby guesthouses to order the proprietors "to have trout for 25 people ready, and also to lay in a supply of fresh butter and bread," so that, strengthened by a good meal, they could wander in the valley.

The picturesque limestone cliffs between Erkrath and Mettmann were formed in the Devonian Age, between 360 and 410 million years ago. At

2

that time, a shallow, tropically-warm sea covered the area that is now central and southern Europe. Clay and sand were repeatedly washed into the sea and laid down layer by layer. Coral reefs developed that, with the remains of their former occupants (lime-containing shells), created enormous chalk layers over the course of millions of years, finally hardening into limestone. These layers were covered over with slate. Finally, more clay and sand were washed into the sea from the land during the later Devonian Age, destroying the coral reefs' habitat. In the following Carboniferous Era (360–290 million years BP [before the present]), tectonic plate movements pushed the limestone up through the slate layers above it. The limestone cliffs became solid land; their surface eroded and was cleared away by natural processes like rain and wind. Less natural was the demolition carried out by humans millions of years later. This landscape of cliffs and caves, where the study of primordial humankind (paleoanthropology) was born, has now to a large extent vanished.

In less than fifty years a limestone quarry that was opened in the region destroyed the picturesque valley and its gold-white limestone cliffs and caves. Johann Carl Fuhlrott, the first preserver of the Neanderthal bones that two quarry workers found in 1856, both lamented and welcomed this circumstance in his first description of the fossils:

> . . . the thoughtful nature lover will doubtless lament that the unstoppable industrial progress of our age has not restrained itself from sweeping through the rare charms of this little landscape and in part destroying them. He will join to his laments the deeply felt wish that at least the part of the right side of the gorge in which the Neanderthal cave lies, which has remained intact so far, should be preserved for the present generation and for posterity. But, however much people may share in these laments and wishes, they should not fail to appreciate that without the limestone quarrying set in train by the Neander Valley Corporation for the Marble Industry on the left bank of the Düssel, the interesting discovery in question would not have come to scientific attention for a long time, if ever.

When the bones were uncovered, the credit for keeping them from being dumped into the Little Feldhof Grotto along with the limestone rubble goes to Wilhelm Beckershoff, owner of the quarry in the Neander Valley. Guided by a hunch that what had been found were the fossil bones of cave bears, he had the fragments collected from the loose rubble. At that time, fossil animal bones were no longer a novelty. Johann Heinrich Merck of Darmstadt, a good friend of Goethe, collected, described, and reconstructed fossil animals. And the Bonn geologist Johann Jakob Noeggerath, who visited the Neander Valley and its cave-filled landscape, wrote:

> The clay of caves, doubtless deposited in what scientists call the Diluvian Period of the earth, appears not to have been examined yet. By analogy to similar deposits in other limestone caves it is not improbable that in these one could find primordial animal bones of cave bears, hyenas, wolverines, and the like. This makes excavation of this clay appear highly advisable, since perhaps with a lucky find natural historical collections could be enriched.

As prophesied by Noeggerath, it became clear how fortunate the quarry-owner Beckershoff's find was when his partner Friedrich Wilhelm Pieper gave the bones to the zealous fossil collector Fuhlrott. Fuhlrott, a teacher in Eberfeld, was a child of his age. He knew about the latest findings in the new sciences of geology, archaeology, and paleontology, and did not hesitate long with his assessment. He labeled the bones that had been given him as supposedly those of cave bears—a skull cap, a fragment of a right shoulder blade, a right clavicle, as well as right and left humerus, two ulnas, a radius, five rib fragments, the left half of a pelvis, and two femurs—as unequivocally human (Figure 1).

Stimulated by the sketchy media report about the early humans, who must have belonged "to the race of the flat-heads, who still live today in the American West," two Bonn anatomy professors contacted Fuhlrott. These men, Hermann Schaaffhausen and Franz Josef Carl Mayer, were curious about the discovery and asked Fuhlrott to send them the precious bones. Fuhlrott kept the two scholars dangling for a bit, then traveled to Bonn himself, carrying the Neanderthal in his luggage, carefully packed in a wooden chest. Mayer, sick in bed at the time of Fuhlrott's visit, missed the first scientific encounter with the Neanderthal. Nonetheless, the fossils found themselves in good hands with Schaaffhausen. He himself had already written an article, "On Stability and Change in Species," in 1853, in which he discussed the existence of fossil humans. Only six months after this first appraisal, on 2 June 1857, Schaaffhausen and Fuhlrott presented the discovery to the scholarly world. Those who attended this meeting of the Natural History Society of the Prussian Rhineland and Westphalia witnessed a major historical moment. In his essay "Human Remains from a Cliff Grotto in the Düssel Valley," published in 1859, Fuhlrott achieved a remarkable contribution to research on the existence of fossil humans.

(a)

(b)

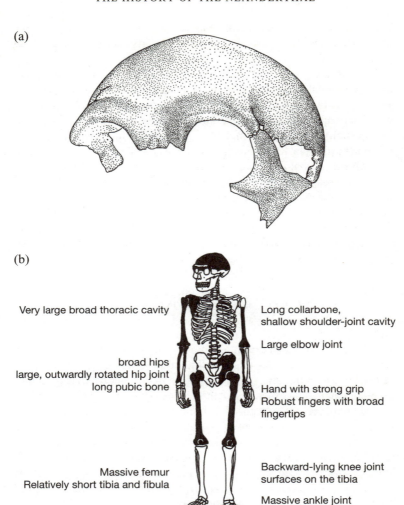

Very large broad thoracic cavity

Long collarbone,
shallow shoulder-joint cavity

Large elbow joint

broad hips
large, outwardly rotated hip joint
long pubic bone

Hand with strong grip
Robust fingers with broad
fingertips

Massive femur
Relatively short tibia and fibula

Backward-lying knee joint
surfaces on the tibia

Massive ankle joint

Broad strong toes

Figure 1 Bones that wrote history: (a) Neanderthal calvarium (skull cap);
(b) Neanderthal anatomy. The 40,000-year-old fossils that gave the
Neanderthals their name were uncovered in 1856. At that time were
found: a fragment of the left temple, a skull cap, two femurs and two
humeruses, a right radius, a fragment of a right ulna, a right clavicle,
a fragment of the right shoulder blade, the left ulna, five ribs, and
an almost complete left half of the pelvis. After the rediscovery of
the original find site, between 1997 and 2000 further pieces of the
Neanderthal were found, including a piece of the front of a skull that
fit perfectly with the skull parts that had already been uncovered.

The discovery would not let the teacher rest. Thus, two years after the bones were uncovered he again asked the workers about the exact site of the find. It emerged that the fossil-bearing clay layer in the Little Feldhofer Grotto was about 1.5 to 1.8 meters thick and that it was therefore likely that the entire skeleton lay about half a meter below the surface of the sediment, with its head toward the cave's entrance. The published data included precisely described anatomical peculiarities in the find, such as the unusually heavy bones and brow ridges, "which were completely joined in the middle." The editors of the society's proceedings commented in an afterword that they "cannot share the reported opinions." Fuhlrott ended his essay interpreting the Neanderthal as an ice-age "primitive member of our race" with the statement that he would gladly renounce "every attempt at propaganda" to convince "and leave the final judgment about the existence of fossil humans to the future." But the German scholarly community had apparently reached its negative judgment long before this point.

THE NEANDERTHAL AS OBJECT OF SCHOLARLY CONTENTION

Schaaffhausen provided exact anatomical descriptions and suggested that the massive bone development of the unique fossil skeleton, perhaps dating to the Diluvian Age, gave evidence of impressive muscular development that in turn hinted at the arduous life circumstances of these raw and wild early Europeans. The influential anatomist and pathologist Rudolf Virchow, an opponent of evolution, took the opposite position in the debate over primitive humans. He personally viewed the original bones in 1872, having previously left their examination to Franz Josef Carl Mayer, Schaaffhausen's colleague in Bonn and a crucial supporter of the Christian creation doctrine. Mayer affirmed the Neanderthal's rachitic bone deformations, which established, according to Virchow, that he must "have walked only in a somewhat grotesque manner." Mayer asserted, among other points, that the Neanderthal's femur and pelvis were formed like those of a person who had ridden his entire life. The individual's broken right arm, he said, had healed badly and chronic pain could explain the prominent brow ridges. The skeleton, he speculated, might be that of a mounted Russian cossack, who had camped in the region during the confusion of the wars of liberation against Napoleon in 1813/1814. Thus the Neanderthal was no fossil, but a recent cavalryman with pathological bone deformities. Virchow, founder of the German Progress Party, socialist, and political opponent of evolution theory as an elitist idea of the natural partiality of a "race," could only support this interpretation. As he said: "The Neanderthal skull should provisionally be regarded only as a remarkable unique appearance. Until we gain further enlightenment from parallel discoveries, we must hold to the belief that this is a case of a completely idiosyncratic formation."

This thesis of "remarkable unique appearance" was soon refuted. Following doubt about the fossil human find in Germany, the debate had spread widely in England. In 1860, Sir Charles Lyell, father of modern geology, had expressed interest in the fossil find. In the course of a trip to Europe he visited the Neander Valley, accompanied by Fuhlrott, and produced the only contemporary profile sketch of the site. Upon his return to England he carried a cast of the Neanderthal's skull cap in his luggage, which soon passed through the hands of several scientists. Besides the skull cap, George Busk's 1861 English translation of Schaaffhausen's first anatomical description of the Neanderthal caused a sensation. Two years later Lyell published *The Geographical Evidence of the Antiquity of Man*, in which he dealt specifically with the German discovery. In the same year, 1863, Thomas Henry Huxley compared the Neanderthal to the skulls that had been discovered at Engis, near Liège in Belgium, 26 years before the Neanderthal was uncovered at Mettmann (Figure 2). In conjunction with the Belgian discovery, the Neanderthal became the prime piece of evidence used by evolution theorists, because the human bones from Belgium—the skulls of a child and of an adult—were almost identical to those of a modern human. The Neanderthal, with what Huxley called "apelike characteristics," was thus not quite seen as a "missing link," but still the skull was regarded as the human skull most like that of an ape of any that had yet been discovered. Huxley's cautious hypotheses did in fact rest on the false classification of the Engis fossils. A hundred years later, in 1936, the child's skull, which Philippe-Charles Schmerling had discovered in 1829/1830, was declared to be that of a Neanderthal about 70,000 years old. However, the adult skull found at the same site belonged to a modern human.

Geology professor William King's view of the Neanderthal find was far more emphatic. He was of the opinion that the fossil remains represented a unique species of the human family, *Homo neanderthalensis*. This interpretation came at the beginning of the colonial period, when European scientists regarded some newly "discovered" human populations, like "Eskimos," "Negroes," or Australians, as less developed than others. King also thought that *Homo neanderthalensis* appeared too primitive to be classified as a subspecies of *Homo sapiens*. Thus the Neanderthal should receive its own classification. More and more convinced of the "brutish" characteristics of the Neanderthal, King revised his views the

(a)

(b)

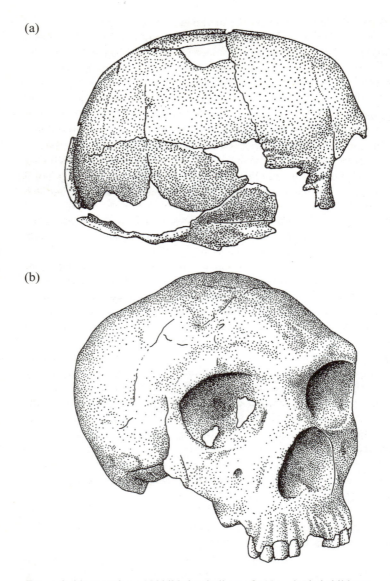

Figure 2 (a) As early as 1829/30 the skullcap of a Neanderthal child was uncovered in Engis, Belgium. (b) Gibraltar I followed in 1848, the skull of what appears to be a female, which is now regarded as an early Neanderthal. The scientific importance of the two finds was first recognized long after the discovery of the Neanderthal of the Feldhof Grotto in 1856.

next year and attributed the bones in 1864 to a fossil human ape. Despite his changed opinion, the scientific classification of the skeleton as *Homo neanderthalensis* survived. The zoologist George Busk, mentioned above, was more consistent in his interpretations. In 1863, this translator of Schaaffhausen's essay had the good fortune to gain possession of a skull that had been discovered at Gibraltar in 1848. The similarities between this find from the Forbes Quarries and the Neanderthal from Düsseldorf were immense (Figure 2). Busk realized the scientific importance of this find immediately: finally it was possible to place another example beside the fossil early human from Mettmann. The Gibraltar skull, now believed to be about 50,000 years old, showed that the Neanderthal was not a coincidental idiosyncratic oddity, as Virchow continued to assert until his death in 1902.

The Neanderthal as fossil human type was a reality. Even Professor Mayer could scarcely argue that a rachitic cossack from the 1814 campaign could have crawled away into the crevices of Gibraltar's cliffs, as Busk ironically pointed out. He was right. The finds from Belgium, Gibraltar, and Germany were not the only ones by which Mayer's thesis of the rachitic cossack was laid to rest forever. In 1866 the fragmentary jawbone of a Neanderthal was found in the Belgian La Naulette Cave. A further important discovery followed in 1886 with the unearthing of two almost complete Neanderthal skeletons near Spy in Belgium, now dated to 60,000 years BP. Schaaffhausen triumphed: "A recent find of great importance, which can be seen as a confirmation of my explanation of the Neanderthal bones . . .." The human remains, uncovered along with the bones of horses, deer, hyenas, and mammoths, among others, and also with stone tools, provided incontrovertible evidence that the Neanderthal was no obscure unique find, but rather should be regarded as a primitive human type.

THE NEANDERTHAL INSPIRES SCHOLARS

Contemporary advances in the new sciences of geology, archaeology, and prehistoric research helped encourage debate about the existence of fossil humans. Charles Lyell, mentioned above, demonstrated the great age of the earth in the 1830s, thus breaking with the Christian worldview according to which people in the eighteenth century still regarded the earth as only 6000 years old. After his visit to the Neander Valley, Lyell classified the Feldhof Grotto man as belonging to the Middle Pleistocene Age (730,000 to 127,000 years BP). The foundations of Pleistocene chronology, the division of the last ice age into different periods, was only fixed through the work of the geographers Albrecht Penck and Eduard Brückner in about 1909, but interest in a more precise dating of the layering sequence was already present before the turn of the century. Animal fossils were already known, but it was only after the mid-nineteenth century that tools were discovered for the first time: flint implements from Abbeville and Moulon-Quignon in France. Jacques Boucher de Perthes brought these into conjunction with the geological succession of layers (stratigraphy)— a scientific first.

The French Edouard Lartet was another pioneer in researching archaeological finds. On the basis of pre-existing divisions of the Stone Age (made by the English archaeologist Sir John Lubbock) into Paleolithic (Old Stone Age) and Neolithic (New Stone Age), Lartet subdivided the Paleolithic (2.4 million–730,000 BP) into several periods, named after their predominant animal finds, such as the Cave Bear Period. After further tools had been discovered, telling more about their supposed human users than about the animals they killed, Gabriel de Mortillet did not hesitate long before he separated the periods according to the tools and the techniques by which they were made. So it came about that the tools from the Neanderthal find in Spy, Belgium, were immediately classified according to Mortillet's system and ascribed to the Mousterian Period (200,000–40,000 BP). Thus the foundations of a Stone Age chronology developed as well as the geological division of the earth into different ages.

Although geological and archaeological classification systems became more complex than they had originally been thanks to further discoveries, these early findings contributed substantially to the birth of modern paleoanthropology, the study of fossil humans. The discovery of the Neanderthal in 1856 was thus the starting point for a whole branch of science, whose modern practitioners still study the origins of our primitive ancestors, the hominids. The Neanderthal (Figure 1) and his contemporaries, who first came to light with the discoveries in Belgium and Gibraltar (Figure 2), as well as the arguments over Darwinian evolution theory, gave the mid-nineteenth century the impulse to understand human prehistory, both culturally and scientifically, in a new way. The history of the Neanderthal's discovery shows how important the historical and cultural environment of a discovery is, especially when the issue at hand is the interpretation of fossil humans. Time and circumstances must indeed "be ripe" for fossil finds of our past.

While the Neanderthals were taking the world's breath away, other human fossils came to light that should be mentioned. Just before the find at Spy came the famous discovery in 1868 of at least five anatomically modern humans, called Cro-Magnon after the find's site, a cliff overhang in the Dordogne region of France. Railroad workers looking for fill discovered the fossil fragments interspersed with animal bones and Aurignacian tools. The bones, about 30,000 years old, made the Neanderthals seem primitive and apelike by comparison.

The Neanderthals suffered another "reverse" thanks to a surprising discovery outside of Europe. The young Dutch physician Eugène Dubois was deeply influenced by Haeckel's theory, propounded in 1863, that a missing link between modern humans and anthropoid apes would probably be discovered in Asia. With the goal of discovering remains of this missing link, Dubois arranged to be sent to Sumatra in 1877 as a military surgeon. Obsessed with Haeckel's idea, he began to dig at a location in Java that, by contemporary views, seemed to be totally lacking in prospects. He dug in a region where not even the slightest trace of primitive humans had been discovered within thousands of kilometers. Astonishingly, he hit the right place, down to the centimeter. On the bank of the Solo River near Trinil, between 1890 and 1892, he found part of a skull cap, a femur, a jawbone fragment, and individual teeth, which he classified as belonging to a new species, the *Pithecanthropus erectus*— the upright-walking ape-man. At first, these finds seemed to solve a puzzle about humankind's geographical point of origin, since besides coming from a new site, outside of Europe, the age of the find was unusual. Thus *Pithecanthropus* replaced the Neanderthal as the oldest ancestor of our species. The controversy that broke out after Dubois' return to Europe and presentation of his finds around the turn of the century show plainly how little agreement there was over the morphological and systematic classification of the finds. Criticism also sprang up regarding the point of origin of the supposedly oldest human remains. At first, certain circles did not want there to be a cradle of humanity at all. But now it had been displaced from Europe to Asia with the Java find, or more specifically to the Dutch East Indies—a circumstance that certain gentlemen of the United Kingdom could not take lying down. So it is not surprising, with the gift of hindsight, that an out and out fake should at first have been accepted as genuine and have fascinated contemporaries. This was a filed-down orangutan jawbone, grouped with modern human skull fragments, and "found" in 1912 in a gravel pit near Piltdown, England. "Piltdown Man" fitted perfectly into the worldview of the time, which demanded a territorial origination point for the human species somewhere in the region of the white "races." The Neanderthals with their boorish characteristics and massive bones simply could not be a direct human ancestor, even though they were apparently both more recent and more primitive than Piltdown Man. The Piltdown hoax was only revealed in the 1950s, thanks to the development of new dating methods. Exposure of the fraud came too late to rehabilitate the Neanderthals, though, who had now been labeled as "primitive." Even when it was hard to prove these characteristics, they appeared to be confirmed in chilling fashion by further Neanderthal finds in Krapina, Croatia. From 1899 on, Krapina (about 80 kilometers from Zagreb) yielded up a total of 876 fossil fragments, parts of skulls and skeletons of infants, children, and adults (Figure 12c). Based on the discovery level, the bones were between 90,000 and 130,000 years old. In his publication "The Ice-age Man from Krapina," the paleontologist Dragutin Gorjanivoć-Kramberger pointed to the fragmentary state of the bones as evidence of cannibalism. Was the Neanderthal a cannibal? A wild, wandering beast, armed with stone weapons; in the final analysis an eater of carrion?

THE FACE OF THE NEANDERTHALS—RECONSTRUCTION AND INTERPRETATIONS

With the discoveries described above, the scholarly world had assembled enough evidence to attempt both an interpretation of the fossil pieces and a reconstruction of the fossil human. Thus the Neanderthal came to have a face. A real fascination with reconstruction had developed from the pseudo-sciences of physiognomy (study of the face) and phrenology (study of the skull), both still popular in the early nineteenth century. Its advocates attempted, using scientific methodology, to establish a person's character based on external features. Hermann Schaaffhausen, already mentioned several times, published one of the first drawings that attempted to show what a primitive human actually looked like. Basing his ideas on the finds in the Neander Valley and at Spy, he had the Bonn painter Philippart sketch a hairy man with a strongly projecting face (Figure 3a). There also appeared, unsupported by anthropological indicators, Neanderthal representations like that of Muston (Figure 4b), who depicted "L'homme primitif" as a romantically wandering noble savage, totally in harmony with nature and himself.

The noble savage model remained the exception, though. Especially after publication of the "cannibal finds" at Krapina, the tendency was to banish the Neanderthal from the human family tree. From then on the image of a heavy-boned brute was dominant. The French paleontologist Marcellin Boule, of the Natural History Museum in Paris, played a large role in the acceptance of this image. But with the discovery of a nearly complete Neanderthal skeleton, 50,000 years old, in a cave near La Chapelle-aux-Saints, a rehabilitation of the "cannibal" at first appeared possible. The La Chapelle site was unequivocally a burial. After all, how could the entire skeleton of a very old individual have remained intact if not because of a burial? Boule, however, did not take this find as evidence of a more or less organized Neanderthal social system, which had cared for the "Old Man of La Chapelle" until advanced old age and buried him after his death. Instead, Boule claimed the find as evidence that Neanderthals could only walk stooped over. This error, based on a faulty interpretation of the arthritic deformations in the old Neanderthal's skeleton, also had a lasting impact on the Neanderthal image. Based on this interpretation, Boule disavowed the placement of Neanderthals on the human family tree. He compared the anatomy of the Neanderthals to those

(a)

Figure 3 What did Neanderthals look like? Four reconstructions of a
Neanderthal: (a) Shortly after 1856, the Bonn anatomist
Schaaffhausen gave instructions for a sketch of a human-like face.
He modified it several times afterwards, and in 1888 arrived at a rather
grim-looking reconstruction. It was soon followed by entire models,
such as (b) a mother with child that was displayed at the turn of the
century in the Chicago Museum, or (c) a sitting Neanderthal produced
by sculptor Gerhard Wandel in 1962. (d) A recent sculpture is that of
a Neanderthal woman produced by Nina Kieser and Wolfgang
Schnaubelt, as shown in the sketch here.

(b)

Figure 3 Continued

(c)

Figure 3 Continued

(d)

Figure 3 Continued

of recent—modern—primitive peoples and especially regarded them as comparable to modern Australian aboriginals. "What a difference from the Cro-Magnons, who with their more elegant bodies, narrower head, steeper and more pronounced brow, [. . .] manual dexterity, [. . .] power of invention, [. . .] art and religion and the ability to think abstractly, were the first to earn the honorable title H. sapiens!" Boule went on to argue, after the discovery of *Homo heidelbergensis* at Mauer in 1907 (now regarded

(a)

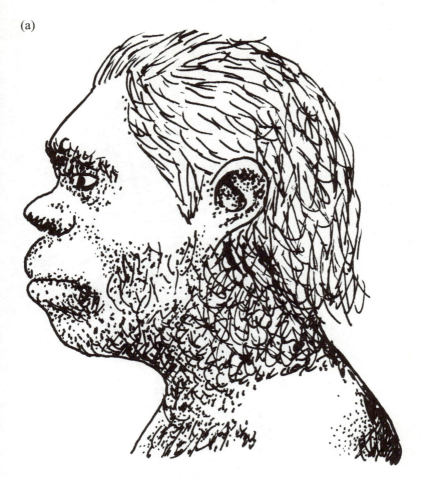

Figure 4 Romantic depiction instead of anatomical study: (a) The image of
a young Neanderthal reconstructed by H. Friendenthal, with its too-
short nose and strongly pronounced chin, also bears little similarity
to the actual anatomy of the Neanderthal. (b) The lithograph of a
Neanderthal that Muston produced in 1887 shows a figure in harmony
with the romantic notion of a nature-loving wanderer with stone axe,
elegant fur, disproportionately long legs, and the supraorbital ridges
hardly pronounced at all.

(b)

Figure 4 Continued

as a European form of *Homo erectus*), that the development of humans lay in Europe and then split into two lines—that of the Neanderthals, which died out, and another, which led by way of the noble Cro-Magnon to *Homo sapiens*. With this argument, there was no longer a question of the Neanderthal being our direct ancestor. It was the superior pre-human, the pre-sapiens, who became our direct ancestor. This thesis was corroborated in the 1930s with the discoveries of *Homo steinheimensis* and skull fragments from Swanscombe in England, both supposedly representatives of the pre-sapiens (although now they are regarded as a typical predecessor of the Neanderthals).

Thus it was hardly surprising that as early as 1909 the artist František Kupka should sketch the apparently less excellent Neanderthal as a crouched caveman gawking wildly with a club in his hand. This stereotype lasted a long time. In 1930, Frederick Blaschke modeled several dull-eyed Neanderthals with stooping shoulders for a museum in Chicago (Figure 3c). Even the Czech painter Zdeněk Burian, whose illustrations became world famous in the 1960s, followed this now-accepted cliché.

The American anthropologist Carleton S. Coon's reconstructive sketches were completely different. He put the Neanderthal in a suit, freshly shaved and provided with a hat, and argued an image of the Neanderthals as "people like you and me." A prominent face, chinlessness, bulging forehead, and flat skull perhaps did not correspond to anyone's beauty ideal, but nonetheless these Neanderthal features were not the "characteristic inferiority or subhuman features" the German historian Fritz Kern asserted in 1953. This was hardly a new insight, since around the turn of the century Gustav Schwalbe had already conjectured that the Neanderthal played an important role in the human family tree. In his publication "The Neanderthal Skull," Schwalbe compared the fragment found in 1856 to Java Man. His studies came to the conclusion that both human forms were extinct and had little to do with modern humans anatomically. These reflections left it unclear as to where exactly the Neanderthal should be classified in the human family tree. But based on these findings others, like the American Alfred Hrdlička, considered that there could be a crossover between the brutish Neanderthal and the noble Cro-Magnon. In consequence, the Neanderthal would have been less a separate species than a step in the evolution of modern humans. In 1931, Otto Kleinschmidt did indeed regard Neanderthal as a subspecies of *Homo sapiens*. The designation *Homo sapiens neanderthalensis*, still sometimes used, attests to this view.

After long misunderstanding and confusion, the Neanderthal found his way back to the human family tree (Figure 5). Yet still the myth of the shuffling, muscle-bound primitive human with few brains and armed with

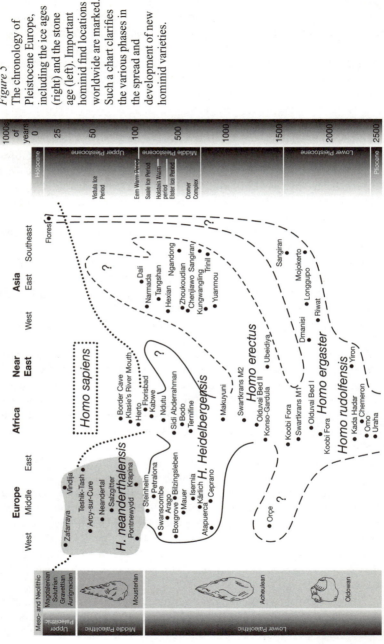

Figure 5
The chronology of
Pleistocene Europe,
including the ice ages
(right) and the stone
age (left). Important
hominid find locations
worldwide are marked.
Such a chart clarifies
the various phases in
the spread and
development of new
hominid varieties.

a club has persisted. The image problem of the misunderstood human can still be seen today, 150 years after the spectacular find in the Neander Valley, and still appears in living rooms and classrooms. Not least, media articles about the "war of the first humans," the "death struggle of the flatheads," or novels with expressive titles like "Neanderthal—Valley of Life" or "Daughter of Fire," which can be called "paleofiction," continue to add fuel to the old scholarly conflict about the differentiation of Neanderthals from modern humans. No matter what knowledge is gained by new discoveries or new methods in reconstructing early human history, it still appears difficult for *Homo sapiens* to comprehend that other humans used to coexist with him, the crown of creation.

2

OUT OF AFRICA

WHERE WAS THE CRADLE OF HUMANKIND?

The Neanderthals, whose remains provided the first evidence for the existence of fossil humans, have continued to play a major role in evolution research. In order to understand the appearance and disappearance of the Neanderthals, it is necessary to take a look at the early history of our forebears, and the tale of their discovery.

Far from what were then regarded as the "cradles of humanity"—southeast Asia and Europe—a discovery was made in Taung, South Africa, in 1924 that excited the still young field of paleoanthropology to a degree second only to that caused by the Neanderthal and the *Pithecanthropus erectus* from Java. Quarriers uncovered a fossil child's skull, which the Johannesburg anatomy professor Raymond Dart soon afterward presented to the skeptical profession under the name *Australopithecus africanus* (African southern ape). The fossil, about a million years old, immediately became the oldest known pre-human find. The small but fine discovery was especially fascinating because of the position of the foramen magnum, the place where the spinal cord enters the brain. This opening was on the underside of the skull and not, as in anthropoid apes, at an angle behind. To be sure, the brain was hardly bigger than that of a chimpanzee, but several sections displayed a distinctly different structure. The canine teeth were much smaller than those of anthropoid apes. These characteristics directly contradicted the dominant theories of the time, because most scientists thought that the purported "missing link" had already been found with the Piltdown Man. The Taung Child, as Dart, almost lovingly, named it, was not the only fossil from Africa. Already in its discovery year, 1921, the skull of the 300,000-year-old Rhodesian Man, from what is now Kabwe in Zambia, was placed in the line of relationship with Heidelberg Man and the Neanderthal. Although interesting for the still sparsely populated human family tree, this find was too recent to be of much help in tracking the origin of our species. For a long time, the scholarly world scorned the more important find, the Taung Child. The "tale of misfortunes" appeared to repeat itself, because just like the Neanderthal and Java Man it shared the fate of being a "misunderstood fossil" after its discovery. In retrospect, the ground for the stepmotherly treatment of Dart's African southern ape was simple: hardly a single scholar was willing to accept the possibility of human forebears in Africa. They would have been more prepared to accept such a fossil, if at all, from Asia.

About fifty kilometers southwest of Beijing the "Chinese man from Peking"—*Sinanthropus pekinensis*—was discovered between 1927 and 1937. The skull fragments, bones, jawbone, and tooth finds, between 200,000 and 500,000 years old, displayed marked similarities to Java Man, including strongly pronounced eyebrow ridges, a flat, receding forehead, a jutting jaw, and massive bones. All these characteristics were also reminiscent of the find from the Neander Valley; the only significant difference was that the cranium attested to a smaller brain volume. The scholars were agreed that Peking Man was an early human, even more "primitive" and archaic in anatomy than the already-known Neanderthals. Could Peking Man have been a forerunner of European Neanderthals? The conclusion was obvious, but it was only the subsequent finds of the Dutch-German scientist Gustav Heinrich Ralph von Koenigswald that linked these Chinese discoveries (which have since vanished) with comparable pieces from Java (Figure 6). He showed that all the Asian fossil humans belonged to the species *Homo erectus*, the oldest offshoot then known of the genus *Homo*. Despite the existence of the million-year-old child from Taung in Africa, Asia was therefore reserved as the original home of humankind.

Nonetheless, one person believed in the original African heritage of humans. The paleontologist Robert Broom, a Scot by birth, world traveler, and research-loving crank, was one of the few significant scholars who supported Raymond Dart's hypothesis that the Taung find was a very old human forebear. In 1936, Broom found the skull of an adult *Australopithecus* in a cave near Sterkfontein, about fifty kilometers southwest of Johannesburg. With this discovery, Broom declared the existence of the new genus *Plesianthropus*. A decade later, he found a skull with female characteristics, calling it "Mrs. Ples." The anatomical features of pre-humans already recognized in the Taung Child were now confirmed with the adult Mrs. Ples.

At this point, starting in the 1940s, a reversal of scholarly opinion began to make itself felt. Countless additional finds gave clear evidence that the cradle of humankind must have lain in Africa. Up to the present, more

(a)

(b)

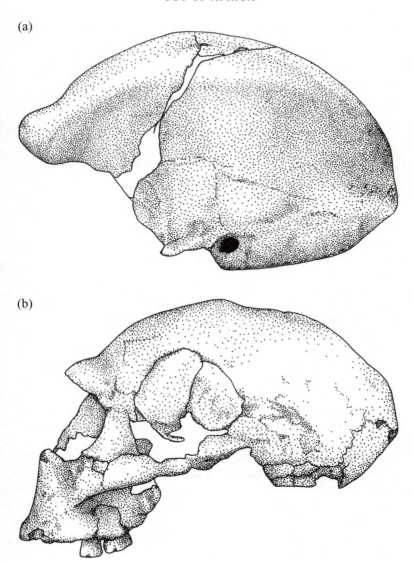

Figure 6 (a) Sangiran 2 is the cranium of a hominid (*H. erectus*) from Sangiran on Java (Indonesia). It was excavated in the late 1930s by G.H.R. von Koenigswald, and represents the c. 800,000-year-old skull of the Asiatic *Homo erectus*. (b) D 2282 from the site Dmanisi in Georgia is one of the oldest *Homo erectus* finds in Europe. The fossil, c. 1.7 million years old, attests to the early emigration of primitive human beings from Africa.

than 500 remains of australopithecines have been found at Sterkfontein alone. Recently, Ron Clarke even discovered the skeleton of a pre-human there that is over 90 percent complete, including the skull, a find that has become famous as "Little Foot." Within sight of Sterkfontein are the Kromdraai and Swartkrans Caves. Robert Broom achieved his second great coup in Kromdraai in 1938: he provided evidence that there was a second variety of *Australopithecus*, significantly more robust than the specimens found at Sterkfontein. He differentiated the new find from the gracile australopithecines from Sterkfontein by labeling the robust australopithicines from Kromdraai as *Paranthropus*. His hypothesis, according to which the early hominids split into two lines, one vegetarian and robust, the other omnivorous and more lightly built, has been confirmed up to the present by many further discoveries. Nonetheless, there is still no general agreement in the scholarly community about whether the robust varieties constitute a different genus or only a different species.

About 280 kilometers north of Johannesburg, at a place called Makapansgat, James Kitching discovered some blackened bone fragments in a cave in 1947. He was, to be sure, not the first to happen upon such remains. Back in 1927 Raymond Dart had heard of the existence of fossil bones that he regarded, because of their blackened condition, as evidence that the hominids who had lived there used fire. Thus Dart described the australopithecenes from Makapansgat as *Australopithecus prometheus*, convinced that he had found the first fire user, the Prometheus of the hominids as it were. Today, however, we interpret the black color as natural manganese staining. In the 1950s and 1960s nearly twenty hominid fragments were recovered from Makapansgat, now classified as *Australopithecus africanus*.

Not just South Africa but Kenya and Tanzania astonished the paleontological world. Louis Leakey started his quest for the existence of human ancestors there in the early 1930s, with special interest in stone tools. He turned his attention to the Olduvai Gorge in northern Tanzania, discovered for the scholarly world in 1911 by Wilhelm Kattwinkel (the researcher of sleeping sickness), and geologically investigated by Hans Reck in 1913. There, Leakey began his painstaking archaeological and paleontological investigation. But it was Louis' wife, Mary, who finally made eastern Africa's decisive hominid find in 1959. Until that point, knowledge of the earliest phases of human evolution had come exclusively from South Africa. With the skull of the "Nutcracker Man" that Mary Leakey found, (given the scientific name *Zinjanthropus boisei* and classed among the robust australopithecines), an unusual series of hominid finds began that was not limited to the Olduvai Gorge. In 1964, what was at that time the oldest species in the genus *Homo*, *Homo habilis*, was discovered at the same level, the ancient humans who had possibly made and used the stone tools that were also uncovered.

Laetoli provided a further site for African finds, which Louis and Mary Leakey discovered in 1935. In the same region, in 1939 the German ethnologist Ludwig Kohl-Larsen found an upper jaw fragment with two teeth and a separate incisor. Further remains were uncovered in the 1970s, now regarded as *Australopithecus afarensis*. But then in 1979 Mary Leakey's team made one of the most important discoveries in the history of paleoanthropology. They had recognized numerous mammal prints in the volcanic ash layer ever since the beginning of their excavation, a process that culminated in the discovery of australopithecine footprints. This find proved that pre-humans had already fully developed the ability to walk upright about 3.6 million years ago.

The excavations of Richard Leakey, Louis and Mary's son, on the eastern bank of Lake Turkana in Kenya (Koobi Fora) have since 1972 yielded more than 120 skull fragments, teeth, and parts of skeletons, predominantly from robust australopiethecines and members of the genus *Homo*. The site has become the best-investigated region of hominid finds in Africa. In the 1960s the first hominid fragments were uncovered in Lothagam (6–7 million years old) and in Kanapoi (4 million years old). Maeve Leakey (Richard Leakey's wife) and her team discovered several four million-year-old jawbones in 1994 and 1995, as well as loose teeth of hominids that were labeled *Australopithecus anamensis* ("anam" means "Lake" in the Turkana language). In Hadar, Ethiopia, in 1974 an American–French expedition directed by Donald Johanson and Yves Coppens dug up the skeleton of an *Australopithecus afarensis*, the famous "Lucy," named after the Beatles' song "Lucy in the sky with diamonds." Nearly 40 percent of the skeleton had survived, creating a small sensation.

With the discovery of Lucy and Co., at last it was clear not just to the scholarly world but to the interested public that the cradle of humanity lay in Africa, and the evolution of our original ancestors began with bipedalism, not with the development of a larger brain. Bipedalism meant that the hands no longer needed to be used for movement and were thus free for other activities. This was the precondition for the development of a tool culture, and with the addition of this it was possible to exploit a wider range of food—favorable conditions for the enlargement of the brain that started about two million years ago. Curiosity and the beginning of a "forward-looking" lifestyle could have played a role for the first time at this signpost in the history of development.

BIPEDALISM

Where, when, and how did an upright method of moving from place to place develop? A look at a prehistoric weather map can help to answer this question. The African rainforest, the habitat of our anthropoid ape forebears, originally stretched across Africa from the west coast to the east coast. Between nine and seven million years ago it shrank to its modern boundaries, thanks to global and regional climate changes. A direct consequence of this shrinkage was the creation of a broad periphery of bush and riverine landscapes all around the rim of the tropical rainforest. This was an ideal region for the emergence of bipedalism by which, according to the bank hypothesis (see below), life on the water and the search for food in it were decisive factors.

With a geographical expanse of at least four million square kilometers, it is improbable that only a single form of upright walkers emerged. One must rather assume that various geographical variants of the earliest bipedal pre-humans developed. It is unknown how precisely this change came about, because so far few finds have been made from this period. In 2000, the paleoanthropologists Brigitte Senut and Martin Pickford published fossil fragments of "Millennium Man" (*Orrorin*), a six million-year-old pre-human from Kenya. A year later, in 2001, Yohannes Haile-Selassie dubbed the find, discovered in Afarsenke, Ethiopia, *Ardipithecus ramidus kadabba* and dated it to over five million years BP. In 2003, another spectacular discovery followed, this time made by Michel Brunet's team in the desert of Chad. This find, *Sahelanthropus tchadensis*, or "Toumai," as the fossil was nicknamed, is thought to be seven million years old. All of the hominids represented by these finds walked upright, and all three of these new entries on the human family tree lived on the fringe of the tropical rainforest. Thus the formerly popular savannah theory (which argued that bipedalism developed to obtain a better view in the grassy savannah) was superseded as the foundation for the emergence of bipedalism. The new discoveries showed, though, that an upright posture developed long before the spread of Africa's grassy savannah. Replacing the savannah theory was the very convincing bank hypothesis, propounded by the Berlin anthropologist Carsten Niemitz. He proposed that humans developed the ability to stand on two legs in the water. Nowhere is walking on four feet as disadvantageous as in water. A logical resulting action is to raise the upper body, because the water resistance is thus decreased, the view is better, and both hands remain free to bring food safely to the bank. Upon examination of the body-mass concentrations of primates and humans, it was striking that primates, unlike other four-legged animals, carry 60–70 percent of their weight on the hind legs, so that rising to the vertical was a step that could also be accomplished anatomically, at least when in the water. Owen Lovejoy, who examined the famous Lucy's skeleton, offers another explanation. Basing his theory on the great importance of mating for humans, he speculated that childrearing could have prevented females from collecting food. They were therefore dependent on the male members of the group. Bipedalism could therefore have developed because males had to bring food to their "partners." The need for free hands to carry food thus was built on the supposed existence of a social system.

The theory of Peter Wheeler, on the contrary, is based on physiology. He argues that the heat of the tropical African savannah placed a heavy strain on those who lived there. In order to "get out of the way" of the radiating heat, in the most literal sense, the pre-human minimized the surface area exposed to the sun and began to go upright. By holding the body this way, the heat would strike only head and shoulders, while four-legged creatures receive the sun's full force on the entire back and head. One should not forget the earth's reflected heat either, which provides additional warmth to the feet and belly. This interpretation would also explain early humans' hair loss—reduced body hair along with increased sweat secretion through sweat glands could cool the entire body.

However often and in however many places the initial impetus came for the "discovery" of bipedalism will with luck be fixed by future discoveries. One point that can be made from the existing remains of the first bipedal walkers from Africa, though, is that our oldest ancestors, with or without Neanderthals in their close kin group, cannot be traced back to a single "missing link." Rather, they show that the line of descent of our forebears consists of something much more like a broad family "bush", with geographical variants, than it does a linear family tree. The spread of australopithecines across Africa from four to three million years ago attests this point very well, because the different species did not all come from a single region. We will encounter this view of geographical isolation and species formation with the later Neanderthals.

THE EARLIEST HUMANS

But what about the origin of humans? How, when, and where did our genus, *Homo*, emerge? So far, nearly 200 hominid fragments have been found, which should be reckoned in the broadest sense as early members of the genus *Homo*. The remains come from about forty individuals. Today scholars recognize the existence of two earliest *Homo* types. *Homo rudolfensis* lived 2.5 to 1.8 million years ago (Malawi, Kenya, Ethiopia) and *Homo habilis* 2.1 to 1.8 million years ago (Kenya, Tanzania, South Africa). Confusing for scholars and laypeople alike is the blending together of australopithecine and *Homo* characteristics in the two. While *Homo rudolfensis* (the earliest evidence for which, a 2.5 million-year-old lower jaw, was uncovered by the Hominid Corridor Research Project [HCRP] in 1991 in Malawi) attests a primitive set of teeth but appears already *Homo*-like in its walking apparatus, *Homo habilis* with its reduced tooth roots shows progress in dentition, but in skeletal structure is more like pre-humans than humans. Evidently there was an alternative to the powerful chewing apparatus of the robust pre-humans, so that in certain climatic conditions, especially dryness, they could deal with harder food: tools. Very ancient pebble tools were discovered in 1995 near Gona, Ethiopia, which were about 2.6 million years old. New finds on the west bank of Lake Turkana also established that already by c. 2.5 million years BP the first tool cultures had been established—contemporaneous with the emergence of the genus *Homo*. But the most famous stone tools have come from the Tanzanian Olduvai Gorge. So-called pebble-choppers were purposely made here by *Homo habilis* and later *Homo erectus*. Stone materials for these tools, from what is known as the Oldowan Culture, were collected from an area of two to three kilometers and later worked. Was it the first appearance of the human as a forward-looking tool-maker, who despite the unfairness of the environment made himself independent of nature? In nature it was no new phenomenon. "Tools" in the sense of implements are widely used in the animal kingdom, especially among the primates. With humans, this increasing independence from habitat indeed led to an increasing dependence on the tools they used, still a characteristic feature of our species.

About two million years ago a new hominid variety began to develop in Africa. The "newcomer" was equipped with a powerful, large skeleton and a massive skull—the typical features of the *Homo erectus*, which at the time of first discovery of Java Man and Peking Man had been mistakenly labeled as the first upright walker (*erectus*). From our current perspective, though, it is not its bipedal stance that makes the *Homo erectus* significant, but rather its large brain and the ability to move quickly. The *Homo erectus* finds from Java and China already attested to the early humans' large brain cavity. The anatomy of this human type was especially confirmed by OH9 (Figure 7a), the skullcap of a c. 1.2 million-year-old find from Olduvai, and Richard Leakey's discoveries on the east bank of Lake Turkana in northern Kenya. KNM-ER 3733 (Figure 7) and KNM-ER 3883 are the catalogue numbers of the best-known remains of *Homo erectus*, dated to about 1.7 million years BP. These early human fragments were superseded, however, by the discovery of a nearly complete skeleton

(a)

(b)

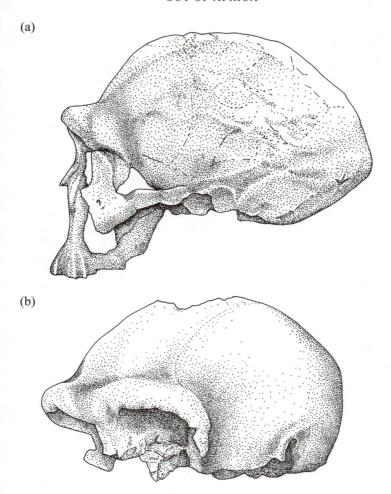

Figure 7 (a) All together *Homo erectus*: the hominids KNMER 3733, OH 9,
and the nearly complete skeleton of the so-called "Turkana Boy"
KNM-WT 15000 show a far greater brain volume by comparison
to the pre- and proto-humans that preceded them. KNMER 3733
was discovered in Koobi Fora, Kenya, by Bernard Ngeneo in 1975;
with an age of 1.75 million years, it numbers among the early *Homo
erectus* (*Homo ergaster*). (b) In 1960, Louis Leakey had already found
the 1.4 million-year-old OH 9 in the Olduvai Gorge of Tanzania, a
skullcap with massive supraorbital ridges and a brain volume of over
1000 cm³. (c) The 1.50-meter tall skeleton of "Turkana Boy" was
discovered near Nariokotome, West Turkana, Kenya, in 1984. With
an age of 1.6 million years, it is the most complete skeleton of an early
human that has been discovered.

(c)

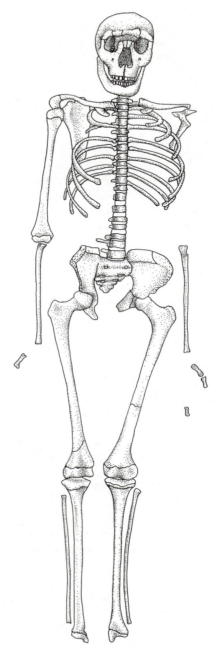

Figure 7 Continued

at Nariokotome on the west bank of Lake Turkana (Figure 7b). The fossil bone, skull, and tooth characteristics allowed those investigating the skeleton to determine that the individual was only twelve years old at time of death. The "Nariokotome Boy" or "Turkana Boy" was notably tall for his age, a full 1.62 meters at the time of his death. He was a giant by comparison to the pre-human adult Lucy, who was only 1.30 meters tall. The height made sense, because longer legs made it possible for *Homo erectus* to be more active—crossing savannah, hunting, and possibly running.

The increasing body size and improved motor skills in human evolution go hand in hand with the enlargement and specialization of the brain. The slow enlargement of the thought organ from the pre-human *Australopithecus* brain to that of the early human *Homo erectus* is notable. The brain volume of a Nutcracker Man measured only 400–500 cubic centimeters, the "Able Man" (*Homo habilis*) between 500 and 800, and the *Homo erectus* between 700 and 1300 cubic centimeters. The size of the brain nearly tripled, with the consequence still seen today of a large skullcap. A reason for this "memorable" development in human evolution might, among other causes, have been fights for precedence and the emergence of social behaviors, which gave humans enough "food for thought" to develop further. A less speculative explanation can be found in prehistoric cooking. The "discovery" of fire and the invention of stone tools revolutionized our ancestors' Pleistocene menu. Meat—freshly killed or the leftovers scavenged from carnivores' meals—became part of our forebears' diet and, as a source of protein, significantly increased the potential for brain growth.

The purposeful use of fire can be seen starting about 1.5 to 1.2 million years ago. By comparing the burn traces on bones in a bush fire and in a cooking fire, the first controlled use of fire can be proven at the South African site Swartkrans. The mastery of fire certainly presented the early human *Homo erectus* with a challenge that led to a functioning social order. For it was desirable to transport, regularly stoke, and control fire so it could serve as protection against wild animals, provide warmth, or serve as "kitchen helper." Both the ability to use fire and early humans' ability to make tools were the preconditions for the next chapter in human history, when the human being left Africa and conquered the "Old World."

EARLY HUMANS OUTSIDE OF AFRICA

The oldest early human fossils outside of Africa, found in Java (Mojokerto, Sangiran, Figure 6a) and China (Longgupo Cave in Szechuan), are, according to new dating methods, about 1.8 million years old. A similar age has been proposed for the stone tools found at Orçe in southern Spain. The skulls and lower jaws of the hominid finds at Dmanisi in Georgia are only slightly younger (Figure 6b). In northern Israel, though, excavators have unearthed stone tools that are over two million years old. It was thus, at the latest, at this time that the early *Homo erectus* or a later, not yet archaeologically attested, *Homo rudolfensis* first left the African continent (see Figure 18). Where their wanderings led them first can only be settled conclusively by future fossil discoveries. At the present it is already clear, nonetheless, that our ancestors left Africa in at least two expansion phases— roughly two million and one million years ago, and at that time they used existing spits of land or the shallow sea level not just to sight a new land but also to settle (see the Appendix, Figure 23). Sardinia, Gibraltar, Greece, and the Near East could all have served as possible bridgeheads for the curious early humans in their emigration to Asia and Europe.

During the first expansion of about two million years ago, the early humans reached southeast Asia, the Near East and Black Sea region, Georgia, southern Spain, and the Levant (see Figure 18). About one million years ago they pushed further and "discovered" central Europe and northern China. In these regions, long cold periods alternated with brief warm spells; climate and living conditions were very different from the African habitat of the first primitive humans. By, at the latest, 500,000 years ago, *Homo erectus* had settled beyond Africa in east Asia, southeast Asia, and central and southern Europe—despite ice-age climatic fluctuations in some regions. The humans, with their technical and cultural developments, faced new challenges in their new habitats. Thus in the entire Old World the last evolutionary step on the way to modern humans commenced—the transition to "archaic *Homo sapiens*."

This term is used to describe the transition from the development stage of early humans to that of modern humans. As with the early pre-humans in Africa, "archaic *Homo sapiens*" existed in various, thus geographical, variants depending on where they settled. The Neanderthals sprang from the European variant of the early human *Homo erectus*—called *Homo heidelbergensis*. As the first discovered fossil ancestors, before their recognition as a self-standing human species, they were initially renowned, then misunderstood, and finally recognized in their special position on the human family "bush". For many years, recognition of the development of variants played almost no role in the interpretation of hominid fossils—it was only the age that mattered. Thus the discovery of the first human fossil in Africa, at Kabwe in Zambia, led Arthur Smith Woodward, an expert on fish fossils at the British Museum, to prophesy in 1921 that this skull might give a new lease on life to the idea that the Neanderthal was the true ancestor of *Homo sapiens*. The skullcap uncovered in Ngandong, Java, between 1931 and 1933 was even classified as a "tropical Neanderthal." Today the classifications of the two finds oscillate between *Homo erectus* and forerunners of *Homo sapiens*; a relationship to the Neanderthals is no longer even mentioned as a possibility. For the present understanding of the Neanderthals, this means that the European Neanderthals also constituted only a geographically limited group, contemporary with other geographical variants of "archaic *Homo sapiens*," which appeared for example in Africa and southeast Asia. As we will see, modern humans, *Homo sapiens*, apparently finally emerged not in Europe nor in Asia, but in Africa.

At any rate, it is certain that the Neanderthals and the still-existing human species, *Homo sapiens*, encountered one another in the Near East about 80,000 years ago. In that region they must have lived near and perhaps also with each other for about 50,000 years, until the Neanderthals vanished without a trace about 27,000 years ago. This sudden disappearance naturally raises questions for us modern humans. It is hard to be at ease with the thought that we had another human species as neighbors, even if they died out. The early modern humans who came out of Africa were nonetheless witnesses of both phenomena. Probably the Neanderthals and *Homo sapiens* were very similar in lifestyle. Both more or less successfully populated inhospitable landscapes, hunted, gathered, developed tool cultures, propagated, and buried the members of their own species. Key to evolutionary success is rate of reproduction. With an estimated population density of roughly 10,000 inhabitants, only two more Neanderthals had to die than were born per year for the species to die out in a surprisingly short time. This is one possible model for understanding the extinction of the Neanderthals. However, it is certain that the Neanderthals' end can by no means be attributed to a more limited intelligence. New studies of ontogenesis, the growth of an individual from egg to adult human, provide evidence that the Neanderthal wasn't such a brute as he used to be regarded. A study has compared the developmental speed of *Homo erectus*, Neanderthals, and *Homo sapiens*. The evidence, obtained by study of dental enamel, in which growth rate can be read down to the day, is unmistakable: *Homo erectus*, the evolutionary sprinter in terms of brain growth and fine motor skills, shows evidence of very rapid growth, while Neanderthals and *Homo sapiens* grow very slowly in childhood. This means that the offspring of *Homo erectus*, like chimpanzees, were born with a relatively large brain. Neanderthal babies, however—like those of modern humans—came into the world more "incompetent." Thus, the offspring of Neanderthals and modern humans were and are dependent for a very long time on social assistance and parental care. This finding revolutionized our picture of Neanderthals. They must have lived in fixed social structures, like us, because otherwise they would not have been able to provide the necessary care for their children. Possibly our common roots reach back to the period more than a million years ago, when the Neanderthals' forebears left Africa and our ancestors stayed there a while longer.

The man from the Neander Valley is thus not so alien as was for a long time assumed. The misunderstandings and confusions about the Neanderthal find and the wealth of geographical variety among our ancestors show above all that the science of paleoanthropology, which seeks to solve the puzzle of the human past, is also a historical process. It has undergone change and has been influenced more by subjective factors than by objective ones. No family tree can be regarded as linear or even static. With every new discovery, every newly tested technique for investigating fossils, the window to the early era of humankind opens a crack wider and gives insight into a long-vanished world. For all who are concerned with the fascinating topic of their own origins, this insight is an encouragement always to be open to new ideas and to remain flexible while developing theses and assumptions about early human history. This applies also to research into the Neanderthals, who, with more than 300 individual finds of their fossil species, have been more intensively studied by scholars than any other.

3

THE SETTLEMENT OF THE "NEW WORLD"

THE FIRST EUROPEANS' ENVIRONMENT AND HABITAT

Herds of elephants, sparse deciduous forests, roaring lions, and grazing hippopotami—the African "emigrants'" new home must at first sight have appeared quite familiar. Southern Europe's climate, at the time of the first human settlement about two million years ago, differed only superficially from that of Africa. Fossil sites in southern Spain, Israel, and Georgia bear witness to the first human arrivals in Europe. The first traces in central and southern Europe appear only a million years later. The famous *Homo heidelbergensis* jawbone from Mauer (Figure 9a), a child's skull from Atapuerca, Spain (Gran Dolina), and skull fragments from Ceprano in Italy declare the further spread of early humans in Europe. The gap in finds of nearly a million years in Europe's settlement history can perhaps be explained by the worsening climate of that era. The Pleistocene ice age, which began 2.4 million years ago, at first offered the early African immigrants a warm climate. In the course of the ice age, though, Europe's environment and habitat changed so greatly that a variant hominid type slowly developed from the original Africans—the Neanderthals. They were the first humans who knew how to defy the cold periods of the ice age. Neanderthals hunted mammoths, the ice-age elephants, ate their meat and also utilized their pelts, leather, tendons, and bones, as can be shown from fossil finds. There are no parallel finds for the early European *Homo erectus*, the *Homo heidelbergensis*, from Europe's ice-age animal world.

Up to the current age, the Holocene, which began about 11,000 years ago, humans in Europe were exposed to the ice age's fluctuations in climate and environment. This was a great challenge, as there were as many as twenty cooling and warming cycles (see Figure 8a). The Neanderthals were flexible enough to survive through the cold periods and not weaken in the warm periods; from the modern perspective this appears to be a

(a)

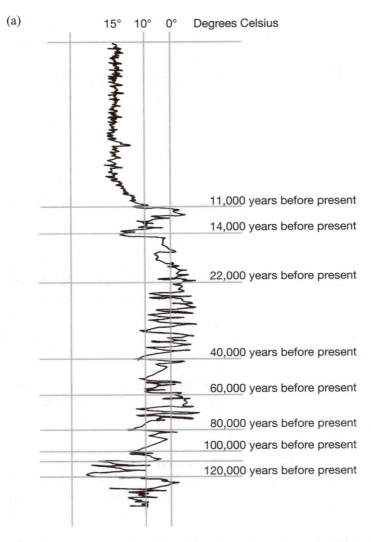

Figure 8 (a) The graph above illustrates the great fluctuation in the earth's temperatures in terms of average annual temperature Celsius. (b) The animal life of the ice-age warm period included, among others, wild pigs, water buffalo, wolves, fallow deer, wild horses, brown bears, and aurochs. After a successful hunt, these animals provided food for humans in ice-age Europe. (c) In the cold period the Neanderthals shared their hunting ground, depending on region, above all with elk, wild horses, bison, muskoxen, woolly rhinoceroses, mammoths, and cave bears.

(b)

Figure 8 Continued

(c)

Figure 8 Continued

considerable step forward in human evolution. During the cold periods, ice covered mountains and the poles, and glaciers advanced from Ireland and Scotland over northern Germany as far as the region of modern Berlin (see the Appendix, Figure 23). The areas of Europe that were accessible to humans repeatedly fluctuated in the period after the first wave of settlement, thanks to the changing climate. To be sure, in the cold periods the area covered by ice was greater and many areas were beset with permafrost, but at the same time the sea level receded, since vast amounts of water were converted into ice. Thus, newly habitable land appeared along the coasts (see Figure 23).

But how do we know today what the world of the Neanderthals and their neighbors looked like at that time? One way to reconstruct the climate of the past is through fossil finds of animals. Cave bears, mammoths, musk-oxen, and reindeer spread in the cold periods. By contrast, beaver, hippopotami, and wild boar only dispersed into northern and central Europe in the warm phases. Altogether, it is estimated that at least 44 large mammals existed in Europe at that time, 31 of them herbivores (Figure 8b and e).

Another method to determine the climate of past epochs is to study micro-organisms, such as foraminifera, hard-shelled organisms that live in the sea. These one-celled organisms build their shells of different oxygen isotopes, depending on the temperature of the water. When the polar ice caps become larger (in other words, the climate gets colder), foraminifera have a higher proportion of the lighter oxygen isotope ^{16}O— a process that, after the organism's death, provides valuable evidence for science. The diminutive skeleton sinks, along with many similar species, to the sea bottom, forms beds in the slime, and finally becomes stone. By boring core samples, it has become possible to reconstruct the climate changes of the ice age with barely a gap, with the help of sediment sequencing—at least for the earth's surface that was covered by oceans.

For a local adjustment of this climate data, one also needs continental climate indicators, such as spores and pollen from trees and plants, since for the most part vegetation reacts to climate changes more quickly than do animals and humans. Practitioners of palynology, the analysis of pollen and spores, can assign the fossil remains of ancient plants to plant families, genera, or even species that, in part, are still living today. Thus it is possible to reconstruct the habitat of the first Europeans very precisely. Did *Homo erectus* and Neanderthals live in oak forests or in the shade of conifers? Was it warm or cold at that time? What vegetable and animal foods were available to the first Europeans? It is no wonder that one of the early paleontologists, the Frenchman Edouard Lartet, who worked intensively to develop an archaeological division of human cultural history, named the tools found in western France after the animals discovered in the same finds. Thus he came up with designations like "Cave Bear Period," but also, for example, a "Woolly Mammoth Period." This nomenclature practice would also have been logically possible for the ice age. However, the two first scientists to deal with the sequence of the ice age, the geographers Albrecht Penck and Eduard Brückner, chose river names to label the various periods. In 1909 they already recognized that in the period from 200,000 to 30,000 years BP the ice covering of the Alps had advanced widely and receded again four times. This recognition represented an enormous scientific achievement when one considers that every newly forming glacier wipes away the evidence of the past and literally buries geological information. But not entirely—on river banks, gravel terraces can always be found that were laid down by runoff from the ice sheets. Four tributaries of the Danube—the Günz, Mindel, Riss, and Würm—exhibit just such gravel. Thus it is understandable that Penck and Brückner should have used the names of these rivers when labeling individual segments of the ice age's chronology.

Between the four great cold periods there were warmer spells, the interglacial periods, in which the ice receded and the rivers became wider. In Holland and Germany the cold periods have been given the (river) names Menap, Elster, Saale, and Vistula, while the warm times are called the Cromer Period, Holstein Period, and Eem Period. Even though we now know that the two geographers reckoned the duration of the ice age far too short, this was the chronological framework within which fossil human finds, including Neanderthals, were classified until the introduction of the much more precise measurement of oxygen isotopes in the 1950s.

To be sure, the admittedly rather confused naming of the icy and intermediate ages did not play too great a role in researching the life of the first Europeans. They merely provide a useful chronological scheme, perhaps too zealously memorized and tested in school. Far more exciting are questions about the first Europeans' climate and habitat, their appearance and their migrations. It perhaps simplifies the description of human evolution in Europe if one divides the Quartenary Age, the most recent age of the earth, into four parts. In the period from c. 2.4 million to c. 730,000 years BP, the Lower Pleistocene, the oldest attested settlement of Europe occurred (see Figure 5). While at first they only reached the border regions of Europe, about 600,000 years ago at the latest humans also populated the inland regions of the continent.

The early period of the Neanderthals' forebears begins in the Middle Pleistocene, c. 730,000 to c. 127,000 BP. The main phase of Neanderthal development lies in the Upper Pleistocene, in the period 127,000–27,000 years BP. During this period, the Neanderthals populated central Europe, central Asia, and the Near East. In Europe, the end of the Neanderthal era falls in the period of modern humans, *Homo sapiens*, who first appeared there about 40,000 years ago. *Homo sapiens* and the Neanderthals thus inhabited Europe together for several thousand years.

Here we should leave modern humans out of the picture for a while and consider the environment of the first Europeans, especially the Neanderthals. When we speak of the "first Europeans," we mean by that the Neanderthals and all of their ancestors who immigrated from Africa and developed further in the course of more than a million years in ice-age Europe. The unusual climatic development of the Quarternary began about 2.8 million years ago. While the climate became progressively dryer in Africa, a first climate depression made itself felt in the warm central Europe of the late Tertiary. Bushland, tundras, and steppes expanded and altered the habitat for animals. With the beginning of the Lower Pleistocene, numerous fluctuations between cold and warm spells set in. Spruce trees came into prominence beside beech, hemlock, and hornbeam in appropriate cold-winter zones of Europe. In the warm periods, alder, wild grape, wingnut, and bog myrtle dominated. During the "Cromer Complex," the first Middle-Pleistocene phase from 730,000 to c. 500,000 years BP (see Figure 5), the forests of western Europe vanished almost entirely. Humans appear in central Europe for the first time in the last warm period of this phase. Finds from Atapuerca, Mauer (Figure 9a), Boxgrove, and Ceprano attest to their arrival.

In the next to last ice age, toward the end of the Middle Pleistocene (c. 250,000 years BP), the development of the Neanderthal finally began. The central European landscape at that time consisted of ice-age tundra; there is evidence of deciduous and coniferous forests only in the warmer Mediterranean regions. Nonetheless, the Neanderthals' landscape seldom stayed the same. In the 200,000 years of their existence, they must have repeatedly adapted to the changing climate of the ice age. The Neanderthals showed themselves to be multi-talented in adapting to climate changes that included temperature fluctuations of up to 10° C in average annual temperature within a decade. There have been several attempts to explain these climate fluctuations. It is certain that periodic fluctuations lay at the heart of the ice ages. While a cold period lasted about 80,000 to 100,000 years, a warm phase (intermediate period) was followed by a renewed cold period after 10,000–15,000 years. The ice ages were not confined to Europe: the Pleistocene Era had global effects on climate. During cold periods, large sections of the tropics shrank; desert, grassy steppe, and savannah expanded. During the warm periods, with their increased rainfall, the desert regions became smaller again and the forests spread. Like today, the climate also varied widely in different regions. It was dry in the Levant. Western Asia and eastern Europe formed a single climatic region along with central Europe. France and northern Spain in western Europe were a little warmer, although southern Europe, then as now, had the highest temperatures.

But when and in what sort of climate did the Neanderthals first appear in Europe? A glance at a map of find sites and their chronology shows that the direct ancestors of the Neanderthals developed during the 12,000-year long Eem interglacial period, about 125,000 years ago. Their anatomy was not yet entirely the same as that of the typical late Neanderthal. The early Neanderthals were surrounded by a thick deciduous forest of hazel, oak, elm, linden, yew, and—completely African—even holly. The winter and summer temperatures were similar to ours today, with an annual average temperature of about 12° C. In the second phase of the Eem warm period, bog myrtle spread out. The Neanderthals and their contemporaries would only have been able to traverse the dense virgin forest with difficulty. Scholars thus conjecture that their settlements lay on river meadows and at the edges of the forest.

Besides small mammals and birds, the meat foods available in the warm periods consisted above all of forest elephants, rhinoceri, hippopotami, fallow deer, wild pigs, bears, wolves, and foxes. Since the first spears had already been developed 300,000 years before, it is possible that the first Neanderthals already hunted. Nonetheless, a predominantly vegetarian diet of gathered plants like wild plums, elderberries, acorns, mushrooms, bulbs, roots, fruit, or beechnuts appears much more likely. In contrast to game, plants are specific to a place and can't run away, so for the most part they can be collected without difficulty or any major preparation. If the plant reserves of the settlement area were used up, then it would be necessary to move. This allows us to establish that the early Neanderthals were relatively "site loyal" within a range of a few hours, rather than nomadic. Besides the vegetarian nutritional options available, the first Europeans' menu certainly also included worms, insects, larvae, crabs, mussels, snails, amphibians, or bird eggs. Recent studies of the 29,000-year-old Neanderthal fossils from Vindija Cave in Croatia have established, though, that the classic Neanderthals who lived there nourished themselves almost exclusively with game. The meat consumption (known thanks to the collagen levels that lead to a high protein mass in bones) was determined to be at a record level. As far as this particular Neanderthal population goes, it is possible to say with certainty that their members included proficient hunters who were in a position to satisfy their craving for meat.

In view of the scattered nature of the finds, though, one must be careful about overgeneralization. We simply cannot answer with certainty the question of whether Neanderthals preferred vegetarian food or game. The situation is different with our knowledge of the Pleistocene climate fluctuations: we know that c. 115,000 years ago the temperatures changed again. It became colder, and warm-period food sources like fruits, berries, seeds, and mushrooms became scarcer for the Neanderthals. Spruce and fir spread, and the colder it became, the more pine trees became established in the forests. With the onset of the so-called Vistula cold period, the forest vanished; bushy tundra and simple grassy tundra covered the land. The average temperature in July was under 10° C. About 20,000 years ago Europe reached its coldest point, with an average January temperature of –27°. For the animals of the cold period—cave lion, cave bear, hyena, mammoth, woolly rhinoceros, reindeer, saiga antelope, musk-ox, horse, and bison—the climate change was especially linked to long migrations. The warm-period forest had in the past offered a richer food supply than the barren landscape of the cold-period steppe and tundra. Humans had to migrate with the animals, if they wanted to survive. When local resources were used up, the Neanderthals, who appear to have lived in groups of up to fifteen individuals, moved on. It has been established from tool finds that the stone from which the tools were made had been brought to individual settlement locations from up to 80 kilometers away—an enormous effort, which attests to forward-looking plans, trade, and not least flexibility among those who upheld the culture. These finds also help elucidate the Neanderthals' migration movements and their spread over Europe. Changes in locale were not motivated by any modern longing for change, but rather by the necessity of migrating along with the food supply. If each generation moved only ten kilometers further, that would have added up to 500 kilometers after 1000 years or 50 generations. By modern standards, this is an extremely slow process, but measured by the development periods of geological ages it is a veritable sprint. Even though that is only a hypothetical example, it still demonstrates that the migrations of the first Europeans might not have been migrations from curiosity or longing for adventure, but much more a moving along with the resources, to exploit a new habitat because the old had become too narrow, too empty, too dry, or too wet.

Finally, the motivation and course of the first "emigration" from Africa should also be understood in the same way. Two million years ago, the habitats, the fauna, and the flora in Africa were not very different from those of the Levant. Rising population numbers raised the pressure to find new sources of food. The humans had to find a solution and moved—more or less intentionally—to where there were plants and animals. As an alternative thesis, the zoologist Josef Reichholf has proposed that humans left Africa to evade the spread of diseases like the deadly malaria or sleeping sickness. In the final analysis, we can only guess why an early

Homo erectus or a later *Homo rudolfensis* set out for the new "old world," because no sources from this preliterate age transmit information about concrete, individual motives.

FOSSIL SITES OF THE FIRST EUROPEANS

The oldest fossil sites from the earliest settlement phase of Europe are known, as mentioned above, from the period two to one million years BP. Some finds only provide indirect evidence about Europe's original inhabitants, since they contain stone tools rather than human bones. Known for the tools discovered there are the sites of Ubeidiya, Israel (1 million years old) and Orçe in Spain, which has been shown to have an age of c. 1.6 million years. Certainly, the finds from Dmanisi, Georgia (Figure 6b) caused a sensation. Dmanisi is a medieval ghost town near the Armenian border, where since 1991 fossils have been uncovered that are nearly 1.8 million years old. Human lower jaws and four skulls with *Homo erectus* characteristics have been recovered from this unique find site to date, as well as a large number of stone tools. Richer evidence about the users of these tools comes from the second settlement phase, which took place about 600,000 years ago in one of the warm periods of the Cromer Complex. To this group belong the finds from Atapuerca, Mauer, Boxgrove in England, and Ceprano, a small locale southeast of Rome. For a long time, *Homo heidelbergensis*, discovered in Mauer (Baden-Württemberg) in 1907, was regarded as the oldest European (Figure 9a). This find, with an age of about 600,000 years, received confirmation with the discoveries from Spanish Atapuerca. The fossil remains from the site at Gran Dolina, which came not just from adults but also from children or youths, have been dated to 800,000 years BP.

In the same discovery year as Gran Dolina, 1994, excavators also unearthed some remarkable skull fragments in Ceprano, Italy. Their age is estimated at c. 800,000–900,000 years. How far both finds can be classified as *Homo antecessor*—the forerunner human—is still a matter of argument. In the opinion of Juan Luis Arsuaga, the discoverer of Gran Dolina, these individuals represent the last ancestor common to both Neanderthals and modern humans. To date, this view has not won general acceptance. The Ceprano find might provide a link between the African *Homo erectus* and the European *Homo heidelbergensis*—but that is speculation. Less speculative is the significance of the remains found at Boxgrove, England, whose age is estimated at about 500,000 years. The tibia fragment and two human teeth were uncovered alongside numerous animal and tool finds, suggesting that the discoverers had unearthed a campsite. Settlement sites provide the best information for archaeologists and anthropologists to gain insight into the daily life of early humans. What did they eat? Where was fire made and food cooked? Were there already specialized activity areas for tool-makers, clothes-makers, and gatherers? The famous site of Bilzingsleben in Thuringia, about 350,000–400,000 years old, offers a small peek into early human life with its remains of food, shelters, and fire areas (Figure 10a).

There were further *Homo heidelbergensis* finds at Arago (southern France) and Petralona and Apidima in Greece (Figure 9b). Sometimes researchers also interpret the skull from Petralona, with a volume of

(a)

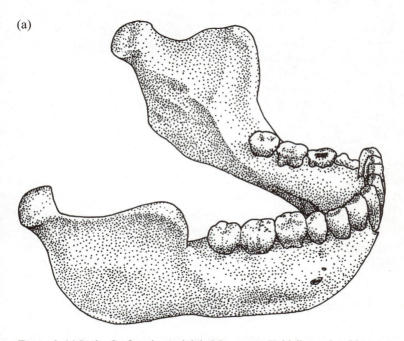

Figure 9 (a) In the Grafenrain sandpit in Mauer near Heidelberg, the oldest
Middle European came to light in 1907. The jawbone of the early
human *Homo heidelbergensis* was dated to an age of c. 600,000 years.
(b) Fifty kilometers southeast of Saloniki the 200,000-year-old skull
Petralona I was uncovered in 1960. Morphologically the skull, which is
usually categorized as *Homo heidelbergensis*, displays characteristics
that already suggest the archaic *Homo sapiens*. (c) Arago XXI,
nicknamed "Tautavel Man," is an estimated 400,000 years old. The
skull, found in southern France in 1971, has a brain volume of over
1150 cm³.

47

(b)

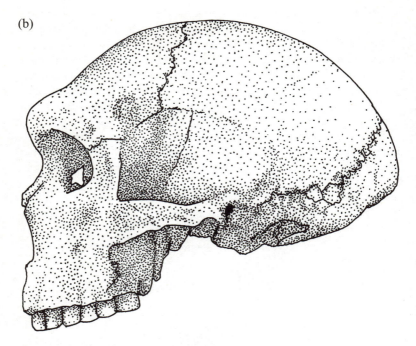

Figure 9 Continued

1200 cm³, as ante-Neanderthal. With an age of 400,000 years, this would mean a very early appearance of Neanderthal forebears. In general, it is assumed that the first ante-Neanderthals settled Europe about 350,000 years ago.

CLASSIFICATION OF THE FINDS

So much for the find sites of Europe's first humans. Next we must consider the division of these finds of fossil bones. Which find belongs in which group? Where are crossovers between two forms apparent? Where, for that matter, did the Neanderthals come from? For laypeople, the interpretation of fossil human finds is a book with seven seals, even when authors and scholars take pains to give brief overviews of the various enumerations and divisions. Next to the dating of the fossilized remains of the first Europeans, their division into groups and their interpretation as part of the complete history of humanity represents, up to the present,

(c)

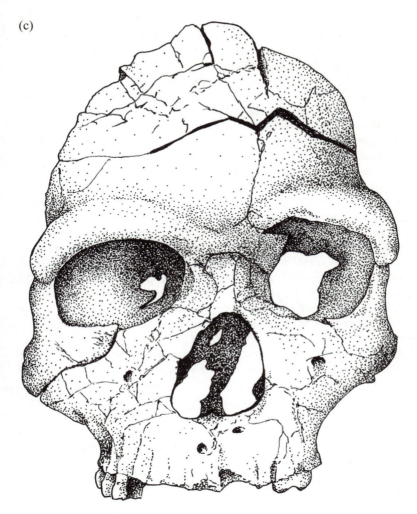

Figure 9 Continued

one of the greatest challenges for scholars. There has also been much conjecture about the age of the first Europeans ever since the discovery of the Neanderthal in 1856. Today it is certain that the Neanderthals were not the very first Europeans, but were rather a first self-standing European human species that was flexible enough to adapt to Europe's ice ages. Highly developed, but in a different way than the modern humans who were emerging at the same time in Africa—that was the Neanderthals.

The beginning of the Neanderthal revolution, the development of the African emigrants into Neanderthals, cannot be fixed with any precision. Many fossils, depending on their age, demonstrate more or fewer of the Neanderthals' anatomical characteristics (which will be examined in more detail in the next chapter). Many of these transitional forms were hence assigned their own species names. Thus there is (or was), for example, European *Homo erectus* types with the names *Homo heidelbergensis*, *Homo petraloniensis* from Greece, and *Homo tautavelensis*, whose remains were uncovered in Arago. The name *Homo antecessor* has been applied to the early Spanish finds from the Gran Dolina Cave near Atapuerca. All of these humans developed idiosyncratic anatomical features and anatomically independent geographical variants. The Mousterian tool culture, named after the French find site, was so astonishingly widely distributed that one can conclude from it that these human groups could not have been particularly independent from each other in cultural terms. If one examines the anatomy of the first Europeans in greater detail—for example, the oldest find from central Europe, the lower jaw from Mauer near Heidelberg—it becomes plain that *Homo heidelbergensis* might be a possible link to Africa. This find, which Otto Schoetensack first described and assigned to its own species as Heidelberg Man, shows morphological similarities to finds from Algerian Ternifine (Tighennif) that are dated to 700,000 years BP, and also to the African fossils from Bodo in Ethiopia and Ndutu, Tanzania. All of them, along with the Heidelberg find, are often declared to be archaic *Homo sapiens* finds. Is the *Homo heidelbergensis* therefore a "transitional model" between *Homo erectus* and modern humans? One might speak with equal justice of a developed *Homo erectus*, though. For if one designates these finds as archaic *Homo sapiens*, the evolutionary path leads unhesitatingly on to *Homo sapiens*. But that is only the case in Africa, for in Europe evolution took a different path, the one that led to the Neanderthals.

4

FROM HEIDELBERG MAN TO THE CLASSIC NEANDERTHAL

THE ANATOMY AND APPEARANCE OF THE FIRST EUROPEANS

Classifying these European "special models", the Neanderthals, is to a high degree an intellectual game. Since scholars spoke at an early stage of "Neanderthal Men," the designation *Homo sapiens neanderthalensis* followed naturally. It, in turn, was replaced by the designation mostly used today—*Homo neanderthalensis*—which best represents the Neanderthal's special position in human evolution. Even though the nomenclature of the "other" fossil humans—the Neanderthals—was not entirely clarified, an image of the primitive fellow from the Neander Valley was created early in the study of primitive humans. The anatomical peculiarities— thick supraorbital ridges, powerful joints, and a large cranium—were already unquestioned as identifying features of the Neanderthal from the time of the first finds (Figure 1). Johann Carl Fuhlrott described the skeleton of the very first specimen as "giant bones," and all other members of the species that have been found are just as massive. The striking form of the skull was so unusual that it would not be found again even in the "most primitive races," opined Fuhlrott's scholarly helper, Hermann Schaaffhausen. Thus it is hardly surprising that the first sketch of the Neanderthal from Mettmann, which Schaaffhausen commissioned, appeared a little raw and uncouth (Figure 3a). Curiosity about the appearance of our early fellow humans was too great to keep artists, scholars, and model-makers from giving the Neanderthal a face. For a long time the fossil human from the ice age had to endure the mistaken image of the brutal stone-age dolt, with lots of muscles but little by way of brains. To some extent that view still survives today. Only after new finds and reconstructions did the image of the "wild man" transform into that of a civilized ice-age neighbor of modern humans (Figure 3b).

Thanks to the bone fragments that to date have been found at more than 80 known Neanderthal find sites from all over Europe, the Neanderthals have meanwhile become the best-researched fossil human form. Despite individual and regional differences, all Neanderthals share a combination of morphological characteristics that distinguish them clearly from other human species (Figure 11). These include physical build as well as the skull and lower jaw. How different the Neanderthals' anatomical characteristics are compared to modern humans can be seen in the fact that the discoverer, Johann Carl Fuhlrott had already remarked, without other finds for comparison, on the flat brow that is typical of the Neanderthals: "The narrow, flat, almost receding forehead is striking," as well as mentioning many other "unique features," which he published in the *Transactions of the Natural History Society of the Prussian Rhineland and Westphalia* in 1859. Today, the finds of more than 300 individual Neanderthals to date permit us to construct a very detailed picture of the Neanderthals' build and appearance. Powerful and rather stocky in stature, Neanderthals, with an average height of 166 centimeters, were not precisely built like giants. They were small, robust, and strong, more bulky at any rate than most modern humans. A strong musculature corresponded to the heavy skeleton. But Neanderthal anatomy was not different from that of modern humans merely in terms of muscle mass and skeleton strength— Neanderthal characteristics can be discerned from the head all the way down to the little toe (Figure 11).

Probably the most prominent characteristic in the anatomy of our stone-age neighbors is the skull: massive supraorbital ridges bound the long, flat cranium and attached receding forehead. The powerful bone ridge over the eyes already appeared in *Homo erectus*. But in *Homo erectus* it took the form of a continuous beam, whereas the Neanderthals' ridges were divided in two and furnished with air chambers. In modern humans this *Torus supraorbitalis* is completely lacking. It is not known what the purpose of these bones was. Whether the ridge played a role in chewing, was supposed to inspire fear in enemies, or simply served as protection for the Neanderthals' round eye cavities is pure speculation. Just as unclear is the function of the large nose. The Neanderthals' smelling organ is marked by a long, wide, and in general large and bony nose opening, and the inner nasal characteristics are also different from those of other types of archaic human. Going from the thesis that today one encounters people with broad, short noses particularly in hot regions, and people with longer noses in colder regions, one might explain the Neanderthal's long, big nose as a way to warm the cold air of the ice age before it could enter the lungs. Besides its respiratory function, the nose is also used to smell. The mucous membrane was further forward in Neanderthals than in modern

(a)

Figure 10
Homo heidelbergensis also lived in the region of modern Thuringia, as attested by the archaeological site discovery and total of 37 fossil remains of the European *Homo erectus* in Bilzingsleben. The early human settlement includes work stations, fire areas, and living places, making it possible to draw a relatively accurate picture (a) of the daily life of these early Europeans. Throwing and cutting tools (b) in proximity to bone remains attest to a butchering place. The settlement age is estimated at c. 400,000–350,000 years.

(b)

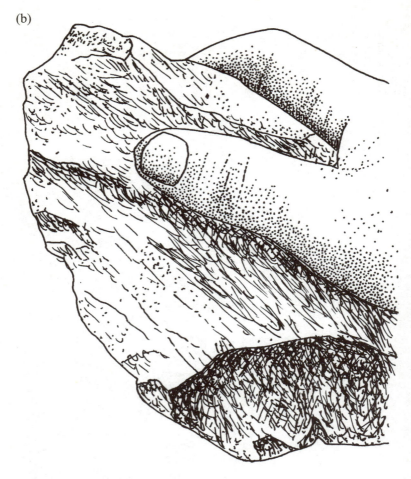

Figure 10 Continued

humans. This improved the reception of smells, which could have been an advantage while finding food, and especially while hunting. The forward-jutting face of the Neanderthal was bounded by a receding chin. Like other extinct human forms, the Neanderthal thus lacked the protruding chin typical of modern humans. Therefore the strength of the Neanderthal's jaw lay less in the chin than in the row of lower teeth, which projected further forward. The first incisors, significantly larger than in modern humans, were used—both upper and lower—as a "third hand," for example in holding skins that were being sewn. Scratches in the tooth enamel

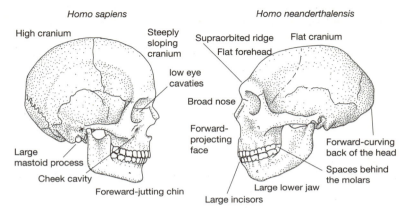

Figure 11 Anatomically different: *Homo neanderthalensis* and *Homo sapiens* display clear differences in an anatomical comparison of their skull characteristics. The Neanderthals' most prominent characteristics are the strongly pronounced supraorbital ridges, the flat forehead, and a longer cranium.

support this thesis. Thus it is hardly surprising that Neanderthals' biting apparatus shows evidence of heavy wear. But Neanderthals did not have to go down to the gums, because the roots of the molars were connected and less divided into two branches than ours. The inside of the Neanderthal tooth had a much larger pulp cavity, which allowed them to wear their teeth right down to the roots.

Much more fragile finds than the hard teeth provide evidence regarding closer or more distant relationship to the Neanderthals in various characteristics. Surprisingly, there are fossil remains even of the filigreed inner ear and the highly fragile hyoid bone, which, despite their small size, provided an immense contribution to research on the relationship between *Homo sapiens* and *Homo neanderthalensis*. The discovery of a fossil hyoid bone at Kebara in Israel in 1983 made it possible to end the long speculation about whether Neanderthals could speak, at least from the biological perspective; or maybe not. It has been firmly established that this hyoid bone, freestanding in the muscles, is the attachment point for several throat muscles. But of course the hyoid bone is not an independent "instrument" that could produce language on its own. It is instead a single part of a more complex structure. We do not know what the cartilage looked like, because cartilage does not survive in fossils. So what does that mean in terms of language? Sounds are produced in the larynx, but words must be formed with the tongue and hyoid bone. The movement also alters the pharynx. In Neanderthals the mouth cavity is relatively high, and the tongue was large, long, and placed further forward. Even though the discovery of the Kebara hyoid bone does not represent conclusive evidence for the Neanderthals' ability to speak, the very fact that the Neanderthals were biologically capable of coaxing articulated sounds from their palate is an important indicator at least for the anatomical ability to speak. Their mode of life, with hunting, cultural activities, and tool preparation, allows us to assume a communication system that corresponded in its specialization to that of modern humans.

Another anatomical feature of the Neanderthals, although perhaps variable, is the position of the inner ear. By means of computer tomography studies, which produced a stratification image of the equilibrium organ in the inner ear of Neanderthals, *Homo erectus*, and modern humans, it has been possible to distinguish a significant difference in the position of the semicircular canals. In Neanderthals, the lower semicircular canal of the labyrinth is noticeably deeper than in *Homo erectus* and modern humans. Fred Spoor and Jean-Jacques Hublin, the first investigators of fossil inner ears, concluded from this evidence that *Homo erectus* and modern humans were more closely related anatomically than the Neanderthals and *Homo sapiens*.

Further anatomical distinguishing features of the Neanderthal's skull include, for example, the lack of cheek cavities, a bulge at the back of the head, and a space between the last molar and the branch of the lower jaw. But it is not only the outside of the skull that displays firm evidence for analysis. Brain size and the organization of the brain centers are important anatomical comparative elements for the interpretation of human evolution. Over the past four million years, the increase in brain volume is one of the most reliable indicators in the interpretation of hominid finds. The classic Neanderthals, who settled Europe during the last ice age (90,000–27,000 BP) possessed brains that on the average were somewhat larger than ours today. With a worldwide average of 1200 to 1400 milliliters, we fall below that of the classic Neanderthals, who had a brain volume of between 1300 and 1700 milliliters. To be sure, the brain volume is always only meaningful in relation to a human's body mass.

There is great interest in the evolution of the brain and in its specialization, since the "success" of the human family to date can be attributed to its presumed intelligence. This raises an important question: how and why the human family—whether Neanderthals or *Homo sapiens*—could in fact have produced an organ like the brain at all. Measured by average adult body weight, the brain constitutes about 2 percent of a human, but requires more than 20 percent of the energy. It is an expensive organ, which must be fed and especially cooled regularly. An improved energy supply through protein-rich food such as meat might have played a key role, as well as improved cooling through a lavish system of veins. The growing brain provided the precondition for humans' more complex abilities. Social relations, language, and developments such as tool and jewelry culture might have come into being at the beginning of human evolution, from the perspectives of both cultural philosophy and sociology. They are only indicators for the final step of a brain development that had its beginning four million years ago. Thus the Neanderthals, from a chronological perspective, have a quite modern brain. Their brain mass was limited by a rather low and flat skull cap. Endocranial casts, that is, interior effusions from the cranium, allow us to determine the existence of highly developed brains with Broca and Wernicki's areas—besides the cerebellum, further requirements for human language ability. The extended back of the head as seat of the occipital lobe of the cerebrum shows that the optical areas, such as optical recognition, sense of place, and perception of color and brightness, were well developed in the Neanderthals.

The reason for the Neanderthals' larger brain might indirectly go back to the climate of the ice age. If one measures the body proportions of humans today and compares them with geographical and climatic data from their habitat, it is striking that build is more compact the colder the climate becomes. The relatively short but brawny Neanderthals are thus often compared in terms of their size and environment to the Inuit of the Arctic. The shorter legs and arms have the advantage of not exposing too much of the body surface to the icy temperatures. Similarly, the Inuits' brain size is larger in comparison to other humans. The size of the brain might thus reflect greater metabolic efficiency in the colder zones.

Even though the reason for the Neanderthals' enormous thinking apparatus has not yet been explained decisively, it makes sense to regard the Neanderthals' reduced body size as a consequence of adaptation to the cold. If, for example, one compares the relative length of the tibia and femur in Neanderthals, Lapps, and Africans, it is also clear that climate not only has effects on humans' lifestyle but also on their bodily structure and their appearance. While among the Lapps the tibia is 79 percent the length of the femur, this correspondence is 86 percent among Africans, who in other words have much longer lower legs. The tibia of Neanderthals measures only 71 percent of the femur; thus the Neanderthals had noticeably shorter legs than modern people from Lappland.

On the whole, Neanderthal bones were far more strongly built than those of modern humans. Besides their general robustness, the knee and hip joints were particularly massive. Even if the Neanderthals might have had no reason to show off with their muscles, they would certainly be compared today to power trainers. One can already see evidence of strong muscles at the bone attachment points of young Neanderthals; this is a sign that the build and muscular development were not just the products of a hard life, but were hereditary. The Neanderthals' muscular structure was created for extreme movements. Their shoulder area, for example, shows evidence of totally different muscle starting surfaces than in people today. Consequently, "sports injuries" such as a dislocated shoulder would have been rare when carrying heavy burdens or moving quickly. The pelvis, too, was built for extreme loads. Although only a few complete Neanderthal pelvises have been uncovered, with the help of the almost completely intact pelvis of the Kebara Man (Figure 14), it is possible to confirm conclusions that had already been reached from examination of the fragmentary Neanderthal pelvises that had been found hitherto. According to these findings, the Neanderthals possessed broader hip bones and longer, thinner pubic bone branches. On the whole, their hip joint was more strongly aligned toward the side—a difference that allows us to determine that they walked rather clumsily. In a Neanderthal woman, a result of these characteristics was that the birth canal lay further forward. This adaptation was perhaps necessary for survival: only thus could the large skull of a Neanderthal baby pass through its mother's pelvis.

The morphological differences between Neanderthal women and men are comparable to the variations between modern female and male *Homo sapiens*. Neanderthal women averaged about 95 percent the height of Neanderthal men. Female Neanderthals were indeed smaller than the male members of their species, but were their equals in robust build. The Neanderthal was more strongly built than the modern human, down to the tips of toes and fingers. With short and sturdy hand bones, he could grip powerfully and hold onto what he had grabbed. The large, barrel-shaped thoracic cage of the Neanderthal offered sufficient room for large lungs and attests in general to an active lifestyle.

This list of differences between the characteristics of Neanderthals and modern humans is certainly not complete, but at least shows the multitude of differences that, biologically speaking, make it plain that we are dealing with two different species, *Homo sapiens* and *Homo neanderthalensis*.

THE NEANDERTHALS' PARENTS

We cannot tell precisely when these Neanderthal characteristics first appeared and became general. Meanwhile, most paleoanthropologists are of the opinion that the Neanderthal might have emerged from a population of *Homo heidelbergensis*. Accordingly, the origin of the Neanderthals is to be sought in Europe, since nowhere else have there been finds of this fossil human type. The development of this unique human type begins with the ante-Neanderthal period, represented for example by the *Homo steinheimensis* from Württemberg (Figure 12a). This earliest phase in Neanderthal evolution is dated to between 400,000 and 180,000 years BP. Following this is the era of the early Neanderthals, about 180,000 to 90,000 years ago. The classic Neanderthals, such as the man from Mettmann and his contemporaries, appeared first in Europe in the period from 100,000 to 27,000 years BP, and then also further afield in Kurdistan, Kazakhstan, and Israel. This last phase of the Neanderthals in Europe also saw the first appearance of modern humans there, about 40,000 years ago (see Figures 5 and 18).

Whoever the humans were who settled Europe—whether *Homo erectus*, *Homo heidelbergensis*, or the Neanderthals—they were all dependent on the ice age's changing climate. They adapted, retreated, survived, or died out. The modern human, who developed in Africa at the same time as the Neanderthals in Europe, enjoyed a tiny advantage—the weather. *Homo sapiens* was, so to speak, a true "sun lover," pampered by a warm climate that for a long time had had an impact on the whole continent's flora and fauna. At the time when the forerunners of *Homo sapiens* appeared in Africa—whether 600,000 years ago with the Bodo Man in Ethiopia or the man from Kabwe, Zambia, about half as old—they encountered an animal and plant world essentially unchanged for millions of years. In contrast, the major climate conditions were less uniform in Europe in the Pleistocene. Affected by the ice age, in Europe it was a matter of larger migration movements and the modification or new formation of our ancestors' morphological features. The Neanderthals, too, passed through an evolution. Thus the typical characteristics of Neanderthals are not found in the ante-Neanderthals and their predecessors, but only formed gradually, until the classic Neanderthals had reached the apogee of their development about 60,000 years ago. Looking at a map of the oldest Neanderthal finds shows clearly that this robust European line must have developed from a single European population. Some *Homo heidelbergensis* remains, such as those from Arago in France (Figure 9c), which were found together with very simple tools and have been assigned an age of 400,000 years, already display morphological similarities to the Neanderthals.

An important find site for the ante-Neanderthals lies in Swanscombe, England, where three skull fragments and Acheulean tools (400,000–250,000 years BP) were uncovered. *Homo steinheimensis*, found at Steinheim an der Murr in 1933 (Figure 12a), already practically shows, with its age of 250,000 years, a transition to the Neanderthals. Its large

(a)

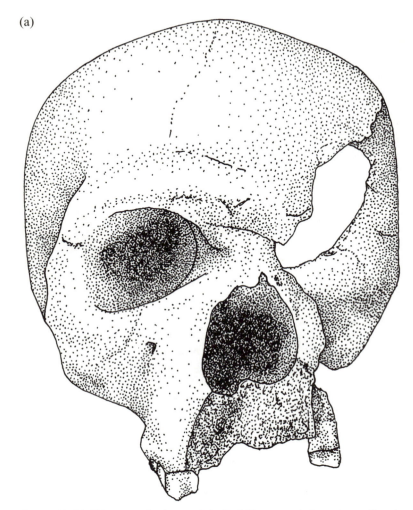

Figure 12 (a) This somewhat battered skull of *Homo steinheimensis* was found in 1933 at Steinheim an der Murr. This Middle Pleistocene man has an estimated age of 250,000 years and belongs to the *Ante*-Neanderthals. (b) The bonecave Sima de los Huesos in Atapuerca yielded the skulls and skeletal remains of about 32 individuals, which are between 300,000 and 200,000 years old. Atapuerca V is the most complete skull yet found of an adult *Ante*-Neanderthal; the lower jaw that belongs with it (AT 888) was uncovered in a later excavation. (c) The Croatian find Krapina III is dated to an age of 130,000 years and belongs to the group of early Neanderthals.

(b)

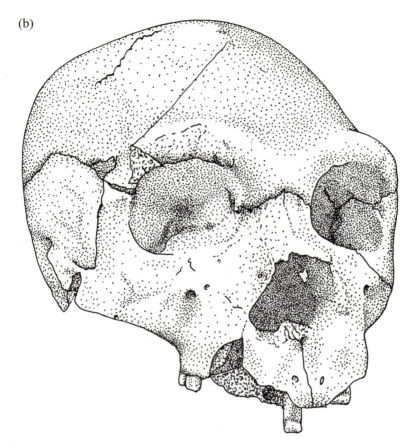

Figure 12 Continued

nose, receding forehead, and supraorbital ridges are very marked, but otherwise the very fragmentary skull is still very delicate and is thus often classified as a predecessor of *Homo sapiens*. Soon, though, a detailed analysis of the Steinheim skull might shed light on this question. Both the Steinheim and the Swanscombe humans were, after their discovery in the 1930s, taken as evidence for the now-contested "pre-sapiens hypothesis," according to which these representatives of our forebears were rejected as ancestors of the Neanderthals. But the Swanscombe skull too shows anatomical correspondences to the Neanderthals at the back of the head.

Finds from Vértesszöllös in Hungary, 350,000 years old, completed our picture of the ante-Neanderthals. Jaw fragments, pieces of vertebrae, and

(c)

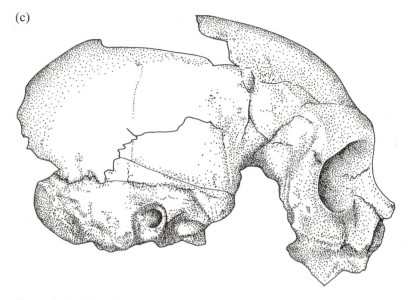

Figure 12 Continued

teeth with an age of 250,000–190,000 years are also attested from Pontnewydd in Wales. The northern Spanish find site Sima de los Huesos (Figure 12b), which means "bone pit," breaks all records. It comes from a find level of similar age to Steinheim, between 300,000 and 200,000 years BP, and has yielded a multitude of fragments. With a full 2000 bone fragments belonging to 32 individuals, this find site was to some extant an El Dorado for Juan Arsuaga and his colleagues. For the first time, he and his team were able to investigate more precisely the entire range in the morphology of a middle ice-age population. Especially noteworthy are an almost complete adult skull, the cranium of another adult, and the fragmentary cranium of an adolescent individual. Each of the three skulls is related to the ante-Neanderthals in the morphology of the back of the head and the supraorbital ridges. The American paleoanthropologist Ian Tattersall concludes from them that the three finds, uncovered in 1992, should be classified as *Homo heidelbergensis*.

Far older, at least in date of discovery, is the German site Weimar-Ehringsdorf. The 1908 discovery consisted of skull bones, parietal bone, lower jaw, and parts of nine individuals uncovered to date. The fossil human fragments were found together with remains of animals and plants, which have allowed us to determine that there was a moderate climate at the time. Today, the age of the find has been dated radio-metrically to 230,000 years; the inventory of tools that was also found is very similar to the predecessor tools of the Mousterian culture. Strati-graphically, however, the finds are classified as belonging to the period c. 130,000–115,000 years BP, which appears more likely than the single laboratory measurements, since this latter date is based on numerous and thoroughly investigated geologically and paleontologically comparable sites in Thuringia. According to this, the Ehringsdorf finds should probably be placed in the era of the early Neanderthals.

EARLY NEANDERTHALS

The early Neanderthals, also called pre-Neanderthals or—more properly—proto-Neanderthals, already display all the characteristics of the classic Neanderthal, although admittedly in a somewhat weaker form. The imprint of the early Neanderthals' anatomical characteristics, today recognized as identifying the features of this type, can be observed in finds from the penultimate deepest cold period in the ice age, c. 180,000 to 130,000 years ago. These early Neanderthals are demonstrably the first Neanderthals who defied Europe's frost and cold rather than getting away to warmer climes. A well-known habitation of one of the oldest early Neanderthals is the French Lazaret Grotto, discovered in the 1950s. This site allows us a very precise look at the world of the early Europeans, because not just a cave dweller was found but, within the grotto, a pile of stones, animal bones, and stone implements that had apparently been placed on posts in the cave wall as a shelter. Hearths and tools that are classified as Acheulean bear witness to a daily culture that can be described as completely similar to that of later modern humans. A little more recent than the cave dweller of Lazaret are the remains of two individuals with an age of approximately 176,000 years from Biache-Saint-Vaast in northern France. On the whole, though, the finds from the world of these really early Neanderthals are extremely limited.

Many more specimens are available from the later intermediate period, 127,000–115,000 years BP. A c. 120,000-year-old skull from Saccopastore, Italy, uncovered in 1925, is among the best-preserved remains of a primitive European; it comes from the Eem warm period. On the basis of the skull's rather light build, the find is regarded as that of a female Neanderthal. In addition, excavators unearthed the skull base and parts of the face bones of an individual that, because of their heavier build, are regarded as those of a male. Like their distant neighbors of Hušnjak Mountain near Krapina in Croatia, the two humans from Saccopastore used Mousterian tools. The find site, discovered by Dragutin Gorjanović-Kramberger in 1899, offers not just 426 stone artifacts but 876 skull and skeleton remains (Figure 12c) belonging to approximately 20 to 30 individuals. In comparison to central European early Neanderthals, they were less robustly built, but with an age of 130,00 to 90,000 years are to be classified with this type.

In the Levant, the era of the early Neanderthals is represented by finds in Zuttiyeh and Tabun, Palestine. At Zuttiyeh a forehead bone was discovered with eye rim and temple. The skull remains have an estimated age of 150,000 to 100,000 years. Much better known than the Palestinian find is the skull uncovered in the Forbes Quarry in 1848 known as "Gibraltar I," which is dated to 127,000 to 115, 000 years BP (Figure 2b). Further finds of early Neanderthals, with an age of 130,000 years, come from Altamura in Italy. Skull fragments and teeth were also unearthed in the French La Chaise; the excavation of this 130,000- to 250,000-year-old find site was carried out from 1949 to 1975. The Italian find site of Altamura in Apulia is remarkable because it contained a Neanderthal skeleton *in situ*. The twisting tunnels of the Lamalunga Cave open picturesque views into the "grave chamber" of a dead early European. This site, discovered in 1993, has an apparently complete skeleton encased in a stalactite.

The find site Ochtendung in the eastern Eifel, discovered in 1997, offers another window into the period of the early Neanderthals. The discoverers of the three skull fragments there, Axel von Berg and his colleague Silvana Condemi, estimate the age of these remains at c. 180,000 years. Especially striking about the fossil is the robust build of the skull cap. With a thickness of 1.1 centimeters, it is much stronger than in modern humans. Still more striking than the thickness of the skull cap are the traces suggesting that the skull fragment from Ochtendung had been worked on. Was the skull possibly used as a container, and worked on for that reason? Stone tools, found right beside the skull piece of this oldest Rhinelander, suggest that this might have been the case.

SIGNIFICANT FIND SITES OF THE CLASSIC NEANDERTHALS

In comparison to the rather sparsely scattered early Neanderthal finds, the find world of the classic Neanderthals looks completely different. Their find sites are strewn around all of Europe, but also appear in Asia and the Near East. They stretch from the Atlantic coast of Portugal in the west all the way to Uzbekistan in the east, from the Levant in the south to Wales in the north. There were classic Neanderthals in what is today Germany,

France, Belgium, Italy, Gibraltar, the Czech Republic, Hungary, Croatia, the Ukraine, Uzbekistan, Israel, Kurdistan, Portugal, and even in Syria (see the Appendix, Figure 23). The uncontested favorite in the geographical competition for the most classic Neanderthal finds is western France. But it would be a fallacy to conclude from this fact that this area was the most heavily populated region of Europe. Trying to estimate population density on the basis of fossil finds and their geography is a venture that can yield only vague assertions. By inference from ethnographical studies of arctic hunter-gatherer peoples, there would have been an extremely small population density even during the "golden age of the Neanderthals," the period from 70,000 to 30,000 years BP. On average, a Neanderthal occupied an area of 20 to 200 square kilometers.

One of the most famous classic Neanderthals is, without a doubt, the one found in the valley of the same name near Mettmann, Germany. His remains, those of a 50- to 60-year-old man, were supplemented by new excavations carried out in 1997 and 2000 at the original find site (Figure 1). Ralph W. Schmitz and Jürgen Thissen achieved the unbelievable coup of not only rediscovering the find site, filled in by limestone quarrying, but even of finding material that had been missed originally, more than 140 years before. Besides fragments from this so-called type exemplar, the two researchers also found 18 further fragments of another individual, whose age is estimated at 44,000 years.

The Neander Valley did not remain the only attested habitat of the classic Neanderthals in Germany. The classic Neanderthals were also at home in Salzgitter-Lebenstadt near Braunschweig. The age of this find site is reckoned at 50,000 years. Besides bone finds, stone tools were uncovered there, worked on in the Mousterian fashion, as was typical for Neanderthals. From Warendorf, Westphalia, there comes a small broken piece of the skull of what was probably a classic Neanderthal, found along with Mousterian tools.

As already mentioned, with finds at La Chapelle-aux-Saints (Figure 13a), La Ferrassie, Le Moustier, and the by far youngest Neanderthal from St. Césaire, France was more than anywhere else the land of the classic Neanderthal. The so-called "Old Man" from La Chapelle-aux-Saints is the star of the French Neanderthals. For one thing, the 50,000-year-old fossil is very significant because of its completeness, and for another it displays all the typical features of a Neanderthal. The "Old Man" is the Neanderthal *par excellence*, even though somewhat lacking in beauty. While he was still alive, the aged man had lost his molars, his life was sorely limited by severe arthritis, and his bones were deformed.

In La Ferrassie in the Dordogne two almost complete adult skeletons and bone fragments of a total of six different infants and children were discovered in 1909; they have been classified as classic Neanderthals. Never before had Neanderthals been found in a sort of grave, and never before had a man and a woman been found who could be compared anatomically to each other. The age of the bones was reckoned at c. 70,000 years. Much more recent are the remains of about 20 individuals from La

(a)

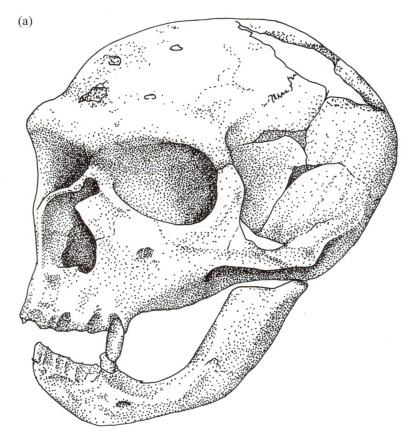

Figure 13 Examples of the classic Neanderthal include (a) the "Old Man" of La Chapelle-aux-Saints, an estimated c. 50,000 years old, and (b and c) the individual Shanidar I, also male, who was already crippled during his lifetime, 70,000–40,000 years ago. Contemporary to the Neanderthals, modern humans already lived in the Near East, such as (d) the woman from Qafzeh, whose skull, called Qafzeh IV, already has recognizable *Homo sapiens* characteristics like a high forehead. Qafzeh IV has an age of approximately 90,000 to 100,000 years.

(b)

(c)

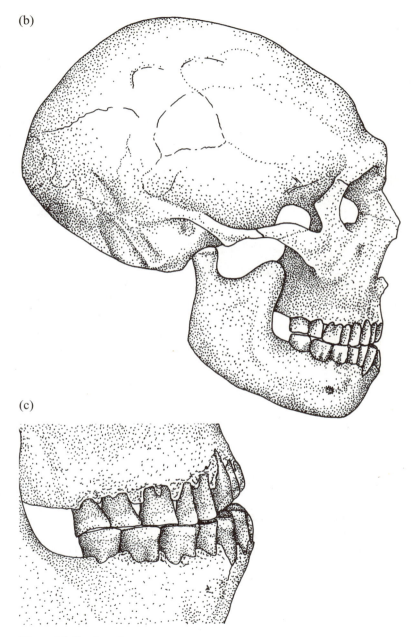

Figure 13 Continued

(d)

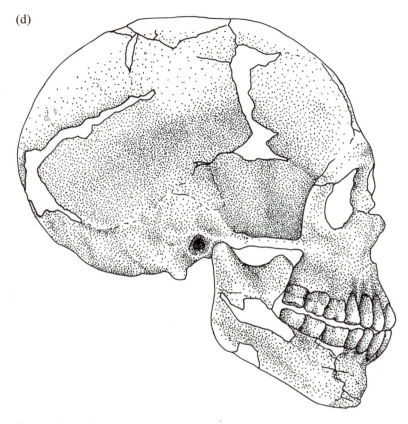

Figure 13 Continued

Quina, which are especially known because of the tools also found there. The tools have an estimated age of 35,000 years and are classified as Charentian, a variant of Mousterian. The name of this well-known tool culture of the Middle Pleistocene is derived from Le Moustier, a cliff overhang in the Vézère Valley, where besides stone tools, excavators also found the more or less complete skeleton fragments of a 43,000-year-old Neanderthal. The 36,000-year-old skull from Saint Césaire was taken up in 1979 as the youngest member of the classic Neanderthal find group yet discovered. With it, the discoverer also found tools of the so-called Chatelperronian. This term describes the mixture of finer and rougher stoneworking techniques that before this point had been ascribed exclusively to modern humans. It is difficult to establish how the Neanderthals learned this technical innovation in the production of stone tools, whether they mixed with *Homo sapiens* or were themselves its inventors. There is much to suggest a technology transfer between *Homo sapiens* and Neanderthals—but which direction this flowed remains an open question.

With finds at La Naulette, Spy, and Engis (Figure 2a), Belgium too stands high on the scale of classic Neanderthal finds. The discovery of fragments of a forearm, metacarpus, and lower jaw at La Naulette in 1866 and two skulls and skeleton remains of c. 47,000-year-old Neanderthals at Spy twenty years later were celebrated as revolutionary finds at the time of their discovery because they ended the debate about whether the Neanderthals were a separate type of human. At that time, the scholarly world possessed only three Neanderthal finds, from Germany, Gibraltar, and the Belgian Engis. At Engis, a child's skull was found in 1829, 26 years before the discovery in the Neander Valley, although it only "came out" as a Neanderthal in 1936. Another "coming out" of a classic Neanderthal occurred at the Italian Monte Circeo. Shortly before the outbreak of World War II, excavators made one of the best-preserved skull finds in southern Europe. The skull, separated from the rest of the body, opened and lying in a small stone circle, gave rise to speculation that the discoverers must have happened upon a showplace of Neanderthal religious rites. The modern view of the matter is less spectacular: that the remains of the skeleton survived in a hyena den, and the arrangement was coincidental.

The lower jaw discovered at Zafarraya, Andalusia, belonged to one of the last surviving Neanderthals. Carbon 14 dating, which determines age with the help of a radioactive carbon isotope contained in organic material, has yielded an age of 28,000–32,000 years. The tools also found at the site are only 27,000 years old. In eastern Europe, the best-known finds are those made at Sipka (Czech Republic), Sualyuk (Hungary), Kiik Koba (Ukraine), and Vindija Cave (Croatia). The fossils from Vindija have been given a date of 28,000 years BP, although newer dating has suggested an age of 35,000 years.

The find site Teshik Tash in Uzbekistan marks the eastern border of the classic Neanderthal's habitat. In 1938, the 70,000-year-old skeleton of a child was uncovered here. What is remarkable about the approximately nine-year-old Neanderthal boy is the location where he was found— encircled by mountain goat horns and deposited in a cave 1600 meters high in the Gissar Mountains. The nearest Neanderthal fossils are found a full 1600 kilometers away, in Shanidar, Kurdistan. The cave, celebrated in the Flower Power seventies as the burial and cult site of Europe's first "flower children," yielded skeletal remains of seven to ten Neanderthal individuals, believed from the find level to be 50,000 to 70,000 years old.

The remains of flower pollen in the graves are today regarded as the remains of voles and by no means interpreted as grave offerings.

The fossil humans from modern Israel and Palestine are regarded as "deviants" among the Neanderthals. Neanderthals in the Levant are less robust anatomically. These were the Neanderthals who lived together with modern humans—although we do not know whether they were neighbors, friends, or enemies. It is likely, though, that the two human species simply lived near each other. Find locations like Tabun or the nearby Skhul at least suggest this conclusion. The three skeletons from Tabun Cave in the Carmel Mountains have been dated to 60,000 to 100,000 years BP based on their find level. The modern humans uncovered at Skhul are dated to the same age. Certainly it was Amud Cave in Israel that provided the oldest fossil humans discovered in the Near East to date. The nearly complete set of teeth of one man, and remains of four more individuals were discovered here in a find level c. 40,000–50,000 years old. With a brain volume of 1740 milliliters and a height of nearly 180 centimeters, the Amud Man must have been a very impressive Neanderthal. And not only his imposing stature was completely atypical. A weakly indicated chin, relatively small teeth, and a slightly projecting face make the c. 25 year old appear quite "modern." Less unusual in his appearance as many more fragments were uncovered is the 60,000-year-old "Moshe" from Kebara (Figure 14). His grave yielded the only Neanderthal hyoid bone that has been discovered to date.

Four hundred kilometers north of Damascus, in Dederiyeh, a Syrian-Japanese team discovered more Neanderthals in 1993 and 1997. The find site is interesting both geographically and socio-anthropologically, revealing something about the classic Neanderthals' social structure. The skeletons of two children, dated to 50,000 years BP, speak eloquently in their careful arrangement about the place of children in Neanderthal society. They were humans who were valued and given burial after death, like adults. The image of the Neanderthal as a muscle-bound ice age brute was revised at the latest with this find. Neanderthals, with their anatomical features, were not only masters at adaptation in the extreme weather conditions of the ice age. They were also forward-looking, sympathetic, and by no means inferior to modern humans in technological attainment.

Figure 14 (a) Kebara II is the most complete known skeleton of a Neanderthal. Discovered in Israel in 1983, the "headless" individual shows, among other points, that the Neanderthals practiced multi-step burial practices. (b) Kebara II's hyoid bone, the only one discovered to date, attests to the Neanderthals' anatomical ability to speak.

(a)

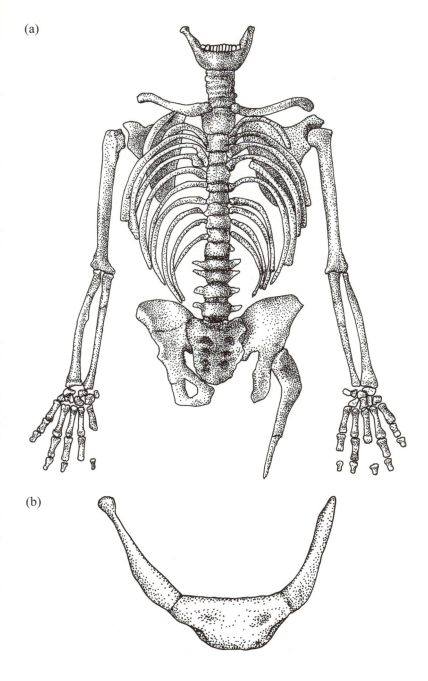

(b)

5

ELDERBERRIES, MAMMOTHS, AND SPEARS

THE LIFE AND DEATH OF THE NEANDERTHALS

The wind sighs gently in the tops of the oaks. A small group of Neanderthals have come out to search for hazelnuts, wild plums, and elderberries in the light forest periphery. It is late afternoon, and children play around the glimmering fires, while the women prepare the meat for dinner and fetch water from a nearby stream. The grandparents, decrepit senior citizens at the age of 45, sharpen the spear points and check the tool inventory at the skinning place. A scene like one from a picture book about the Stone Age—is it reality or fiction?

As human beings, nothing moves us more than our own history. When did our forebears start to speak? Which humans invented music, and when, along with the first musical instruments? What sort of clothing did people wear in the ice age, and what jewelry did they add, to win the gods' favor and shield their sons from harm during the hunt? Paleoanthropology can only supply general answers to questions about the "software" in the life of our ancestors. Teeth show what food was available, while bones can give information, based on their wear level, about an individual's age, possible illnesses, and injuries. Laughter, care, and language, though, cannot be petrified. It is the small remains of tools, birch pitch, pollen, awls, and pieces of jewelry that provide the material for archaeologists, the detectives among prehistory researchers, to describe the daily life of the ice age.

Daily life. What is it? There was no typical daily life or typical environment in the ice age, any more than there was a typical Neanderthal. Some Neanderthals lived on the Mediterranean, others in mountains, while still others spent their lives on plains. In the east they ate goats and sheep, while Neanderthal hunters in the middle west found only grazing bison and aurochs. As hunters and gatherers, the Neanderthals understood how to adjust to the environment, climate, animals, and plant world in which they found themselves. Within their choice of neighborhood they were highly mobile, using readily available resources and regularly moving around within a radius of about 100 kilometers. We know this at least from the raw materials that they used for tools such as blades and hand axes. From the finds accompanying Neanderthal bones it is possible to reconstruct the daily life of the first Europeans with a fair amount of detail. Through finds of further everyday utensils, such as the remains of jewelry, bones with holes bored in them, birch pitch (the stone-age glue), and color pigments from graves, kitchens, and work places, the sketch of a Neanderthal day laid out at the beginning of this chapter seems quite realistic. At the very least, the state of archaeological evidence speaks unequivocally for the Neanderthals' well-regulated daily life.

A glimpse into the first Europeans' living rooms is provided by 35,000-to 40,000-year-old Neanderthal homesites such as Arcy-sur-Cure in Burgundy or the Ukrainian Molodova site. These finds have made us revise the stereotype of the Neanderthal as a caveman: the experienced handworker used mammoth tusks and wood posts to erect a shelter for up to twenty people. Caves constitute only a small proportion of the sites they used. For the most part, when they revisited caves again and again, they only used the cave mouths. Caves offered uncomplicated protection from the weather: there was no wind, fire could be kindled easily, and prey could be stored in the cave's cool, dark interior. But unlike other cave dwellers, such as bear, hyena, or lion, the stone-age human also made use of the open land, where he built shelters. Bones, wood, and animal hides and furs helped him protect himself securely from the ice-age cold spells in such a construction. A c. 50,000-year-old post hole, apparently from a wooden tent post, was found in the French Combe-Grenal, attesting to the building of these shelters out in the open. In the grotto near Arcy-sur-Cure, a site where bone awls (probably used to work leather and furs) and jewelry bones were uncovered, excavators also found evidence of two circular dwellings with several hearths.

The dwelling sites of the Ukrainian Neanderthals from Molodova, also round, have, with their total area of 75 square meters, as much room as a modern three-room apartment. In the interior of the former shelter at Molodova, the excavators uncovered two hearths, along with flecks of red pigment, stone tools, and the remains of hunted game. A mass of mammoth bones suggests that the bones of the ice-age elephant were a coveted material for Neanderthal home-building. Huts or sheds made out of massive mammoth bones are also known from Mezin and Mezhirich (Figure 15a). Open-land dwelling places like Molodova are very difficult to reconstruct for the most part, since bone remains, hearths, and tools were unprotected and destroyed by weather or wild animals after the humans had abandoned the place.

(a)

(b)

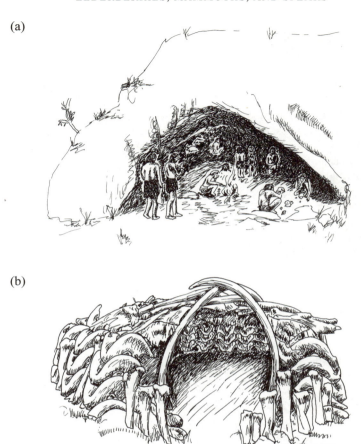

Figure 15 (a) A Neanderthal dwelling might have looked like this modern reconstruction at Mezhirich in Ukraine. (b) No Neanderthal settlements on open ground, like this one built of mammoth bones and skulls, are known, but the people of Europe could only have borne the climate if they had lived in relatively protected places, such as in caves or under the overhang of cliffs (c and d). Figure 15(e) is a reconstruction of the original Neanderthal cave. It shows a section through the area as it was 150 years ago in comparison to what is there today. Most of the original cave was destroyed by mining works, but it was shown to have been in the cliff face, about 15 metres above today's surface, and about 40 metres south of the Düssel river. Some Anteneanderthals appear to have lived in circular camp sites. The stones discovered at the Ochtendung campsite in Germany suggest that the stones were used for tent-like structures erected on top (f).

(c)

(d)

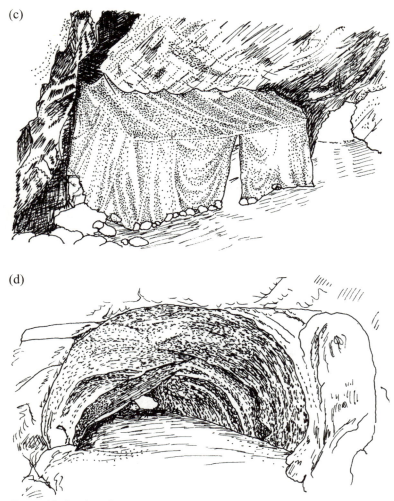

Figure 15 Continued

Microscopic analysis of tools and bone finds, however, establishes that Neanderthals did not just use their shelters as a place to sleep. The settlement places appear to suggest, besides the normal "living rooms," a carefully organized division of work places, including skinning places, slaughter places, and workshops. Even enclosed hearths, like that at Vilas Ruivas in Portugal, were part of the Neanderthals' residential inventory—evidence of early safety precautions at the stone-age workplace.

(e)

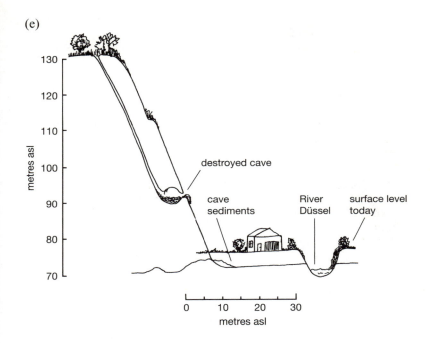

(f)

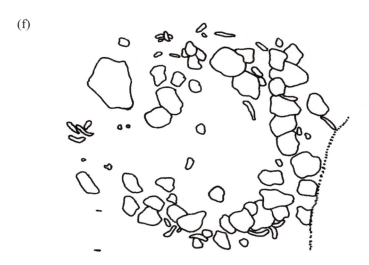

Figure 15 Continued

It is hard to say how long a group of Neanderthals would have lived at a given place. It has been surmised that, on the one hand, they had special camps for brief occupation, such as for collecting specific natural produce, and, on the other hand, home camps where the group stayed for longer periods. It would be very difficult to establish whether this was a matter of a more "circulating mobility"—with regular return to a settlement place—or an outward radiation, in which a camp occupied relatively long term served as a base from which to visit satellite camps for hunting.

It is easier to come up with at least an approximate answer to the question of what a Neanderthal dwelling looked like. The German find site Rheindahlen, near Mönchengladbach, offers insights. This site dates to the intermediate ice age, as we can tell from maple, hornbeam, and oak charcoal. The remains of tools and woods reveal details about the production of wooden shafts. Wood was a quite typical work material in the stone age. Artifacts like the 400,000-year-old Schöningen spears (Figure 16) provide evidence that both the Neanderthals and *Homo erectus* were early masters of alternative tool techniques. Organic materials like wood, antler, or bone were used just as much as flint in the preparation of implements. Traces of wear on stone tools show unequivocally the use of wood for handles, containers, and scrapers. Pointed mammoth bones from the Neanderthal find site Salzgitter-Lebenstedt and the evidence of 45,000-year-old birch pitch (Figure 16), a natural glue that probably connected wood and stone and could only be acquired through a highly complex distillation technique, leave no room for doubt: the Neanderthal did not just have stone implements in his tool kit. This assumption was held for a long time, because stone artifacts survive better than those made from soft materials like wood, but has now been laid to rest.

Because the bulk of our finds is made up of the first Europeans' stone tool repertoire, an especially large amount is known about the techniques used for preparing blades, hand axes, or simple striking stones. To begin, only stones were used that could be split easily and that were sharp along the break, but would not shatter with resistance. The perfect materials for this undertaking were quarzite, volcanic glasses like obsidian and andesite, or simply flint. The stones were worked with a round striking rock made of a harder stone: a blow of the hammer stone on the edge of the raw material would split off stone flakes, in various shapes and sizes, from the stone core. Pieces struck from the stone core that were at least twice as long as they were broad found further use as blades. The worked stone core itself could be used, depending on the tool technique, as hand axe, scraper, or point. Thinner flakes for knives were prepared using a light percussive technique, using a wood or antler hammer, while hand axes, which were worked exclusively from stone cores, were produced using a harder

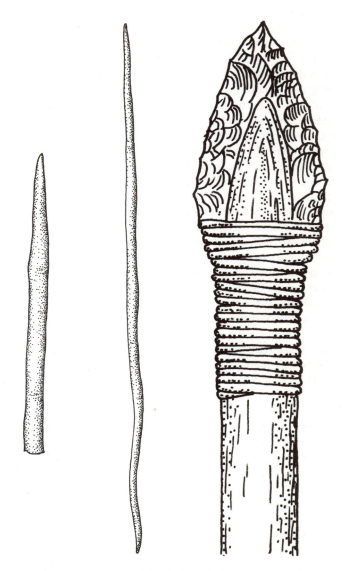

Figure 16 The spears of Schöningen and the birch pitch of Königsaue, which
was used to glue together wood and stone, are impressive witnesses to
the tool culture of the first Europeans. Birch pitch is produced by
making birch bark expand in a closed container heated to a
temperature of 300° C. The Schöningen spears, 400,000 years old, are
the oldest spears that have been discovered anywhere in the world.

percussive technique. The word "produce" presumes that a certain mass of tools was prepared with a technique that was employed repeatedly without particular regional differentiation.

The stone-working style typical for Neanderthals is called Levallois technique after a French find site. Classic Levallois tools were always prepared first on the underside. Then in the second stage of work the underside could be used as a striking platform for working the top and the cuttings were made from this upper surface and then worked further. To get a perfect flake from the now convex stone core, it is necessary to strike exactly the right place. The experienced handworker strikes precisely on this point repeatedly until the stone releases the flake. It does not require a profound understanding of tool techniques to recognize that the Levallois technique was a very carefully thought out style of production that required not only skill but also a high level of abstract thinking from the producer. The fine finishing of Mousterian implements like scrapers and points, accomplished by means of carefully aimed retouching using softer wood or antler tools, speaks eloquently of the maker's aptitude and the user's requirements. Nonetheless, Neanderthal hunters and tool-makers must not have valued their stone implements all that highly. When the group moved on, they left their tools behind for the most part and just made them again at the new settlement. Resin, grasses, and bark for attaching spear points were available everywhere; encampments with flint and quarzite were as well known to the Neanderthal handworker as the location of the nearest hardware store is to us.

The Neanderthal's tool kit was large and specialized—so much so that for a long time scholars of prehistory wanted to classify various parts of the copious inventory as belonging to different cultures. It is unclear whether specific traditions influenced tool production or if the sort of tool production simply depended on the environment of a given group. Therefore, today one speaks rather of "type groups," like the Mousterian, the Micoquian, or the Acheulean, to pull together a number of geographically and chronologically similar tool finds. Find locations like Lehringen in Lower Saxony, where a 120,000-year-old wooden hunting lance made of yew, 2.38 meters long, and some stone flakes were found, lead to the conclusion that tools were made more complexly or simply depending on length of residence and the purpose to which they were put. For tools were not just employed for hunting, but also for skinning or butchering of animals, while Neanderthals used finer tools like awls for detailed work such as sewing clothes.

But even the best tool is worthless when the user doesn't know how to use it. The hunt for large game like mammoths called not just for an arsenal of weapons such as throwing spears and thrusting lances, but also required the hunters' ability to plan, to think abstractly, and to strategize. The already-mentioned spears from Schöningen (Figure 16), with their considerable length of 2.5 meters, were used by people who hunted wild horses, animals known for their speed and endurance—no easy prey. The massive mammoths and bison were not an easy quarry either, and yet Neanderthals hunted them—a challenge that, according to the estimates of archaeologists like Bärbel Auffermann and Jörg Orschiedt, could only have been accomplished by a coordinated hunting team consisting of at least twenty individuals.

Finds from hunting sites like Mauran or La Borde in France, Il'skaja in the northern Caucasus, and Wallertheim in the Rhineland show that the Neanderthals were specialized hunters who repeatedly waylaid and brought down bison or mammoths at the same spots, when they were on their way to their winter pasturage. In Salzgitter-Lebenstedt, the bone fragments of 86 hunted reindeer were found along with thousands of stone tools, conclusive evidence of the Neanderthals' outstanding hunting abilities. After butchering the animals, they transported the best cuts to camp, and split long bones open to get at the nutritious marrow. As already mentioned, meat was the Neanderthals' main source of protein. Measurements of the collagen isotopes in Neanderthal bones indicate a diet that consisted predominantly of the meat of large mammals such as reindeer, bison, or bear. It is unclear how large a role fish and shellfish played in the Neanderthals' daily diet, since the data was collected from inland Neanderthal find sites. Still, the remains of mussels in caves make it probable that Neanderthals also ate both fresh- and salt-water animals.

LIFE EXPECTANCY AND DISEASES

Hunting played a large role in the Neanderthals' life, since it provided the very foundation of that life. The strong musculature of the Neanderthals had to be cared for, if they were to survive the adverse life conditions of ice-age Europe. Heavy physical demands, athletic endurance to cope with long distances, agility in the hunt, and occasional food shortages marked the Neanderthals' daily existence. Donkeys, horses, or cows had not yet been domesticated for food or transport; bows and arrows and metal-working had not yet been invented. So human beings had nothing to rely on but their own body and understanding. The Neanderthals' astonishingly high life expectancy is evidence that both functioned very well. Today, people in crisis-torn Africa, the continent where all humans originated, have a relatively short average life expectancy of 38 years. Thus the "Old Man" of La Chapelle, with an age of 50 years, enjoyed a lifetime twelve years longer than that of the average African today. Nonetheless, most Neanderthals died between the ages of twenty and thirty. The American Erik Trinkaus calculates an even higher average age. Based on the examination of 220 skeletons from the entire area of Neanderthal occupation, ranging in age from 35,000 to more than 100,000 years, he concluded that 80 percent of all Neanderthals died before their fortieth birthday. Expressed in positive terms, that means that 20 percent reached an age greater than forty years, a considerable achievement, if one looks more carefully at the c. 300 Neanderthal individuals who have been found.

Injuries like broken bones, chronic illnesses like arthritis, and deficiency-related ailments like gum disease attest to the harshness of life in the ice age. Many older Neanderthals show signs of wear such as osteoarthritis; and sicknesses like rickets, caused by malnutrition and vitamin deficiencies, are as common as broken bones. The man from the Neander Valley is a good example of the ailments that afflicted Neanderthals: the c. 60-year-old senior citizen suffered from rickets, lived with a healed head injury, and also had a broken bone near the elbow of his left lower arm. Microscopic examination reveals that the Mettmann ice-age man would barely have been able to bend his left arm for the rest of his life, since the bone substance appears to have been significantly weakened by years of inactivity. The "Old Man" of La Chapelle (Figure 13a), too, displays overwhelming signs of bad health. His spinal column, lower jaw, hips, and feet bear the marks of osteoarthritis, and arthritis was noticeable in his neck, back, and shoulders. The skeleton also shows evidence of a broken rib, an injured kneecap, and missing molars. The Shanidar Man (Figure 13b) was also fit for a hospital by modern standards. He was very probably blind, due to a severe head injury on the left side of the skull, and must have depended on the active help of his group to survive so long. In addition, he appears to have had only limited mobility. Injuries on the right side of the body—foot, tibia, and arm—as well as disease-induced deformation of his left knee rendered him handicapped, able to survive only with his group's assistance. Even Virchow emphasized this circumstance in his description of the skeleton from the Neander Valley in 1872 as evidence for a functioning social network: "It is these circumstances that indicate a secure familial or tribal unit, and indeed which perhaps suggest a true settlement." Otherwise, he continued, it would have been difficult for a person as challenged as the man from Mettmann to have survived to old age. Evidence of life-preserving measures like the care and feeding of the sick and toothless old people can be seen in the many finds of elderly Neanderthals, so the old man from the Neander Valley was not unique. Healed injuries even allow us to infer the existence of "medical" care with medicinal plants.

The relatively high number of broken bones in Neanderthals' upper bodies and heads led the American anthropologist Thomas Berger to conduct a comparative study of broken bones in Neanderthals and people living today. His results speak volumes: the Neanderthal breaks are like those of modern rodeo riders. At first glance this seems to be a rather perverse comparison, since Neanderthals were hardly in a position to domesticate and ride a horse. But on closer consideration the comparison makes sense: the Neanderthals' injuries are comparable to the injuries of people who come into very close contact with very large animals. To that extent, the study provides very persuasive evidence about the Neanderthals' hunting practices. Wild horses, mammoths, or cattle were not so much killed with distance weapons like spears as in close battle with stabbing weapons, at serious risk to their own lives. Berger's teacher Erik Trinkaus explains the absence of fossil bone breaks in the lower body by arguing that Neanderthals were in the habit of simply leaving non-ambulatory people behind and not burying them. For paleoanthropology, this means that if they weren't buried, they weren't fossilized.

Besides deficiency diseases like rickets, evidence of wear like degenerative arthritis, and broken bones in the upper body, the teeth more than anything else plagued the Neanderthals throughout their lives. Although among the Neanderthal jaws found to date there is evidence of only three cavities, dentists would have had their hands full in the ice age. Painful gum inflammations and injuries in the jaw region caused by using the teeth as a "third hand" (for example, holding pelts and leather) gave most Neanderthals trouble. Suppurating inflammations in the mouth develop quickly. Even small gum injuries can lead to inflammation, and the bacteria thus introduced are in a position to make their way in no time along the toothneck into the jaw. The result was a painful ailment that could lead to tooth loss.

CLOTHING AND JEWELRY

Even though tooth injuries were a burden for the sufferer, they give us evidence today about the work-intensive life of the Neanderthals, which besides the production of hunting tools was also dedicated to the production of jewelry and clothing. The preparation of clothing as protection against the cold or as fashionable ice-age "accessory" using teeth and bone awls was presumed for a long time. That ice-age humans, whether modern humans or Neanderthals, used clothing both as cold protection and as a means of presentation was proven by the discovery of a c. 28,000-year-old burial site of an approximately 60-year-old man near

Sungir, about 150 kilometers east of Moscow. The grave, discovered in 1956, yielded a total of 2936 pearls that had been sewn as decoration onto his clothing (Figure 20b). Bracelets, pendants made of mammoth ivory, and necklaces of mussel shells and animal teeth were found in the man's grave and also those of the two adolescents buried with him. They expressively reflect the ritual behavior and artistic creativity of ice-age humans. Such a find is especially fascinating for modern humans, who are surrounded by countless symbols in their communication with everyday life around them. But archaeologists find it extremely problematic to interpret such objects as evidence of a symbolic attitude, or even a concept of the hereafter or of a religion. Finds with bone scratches from the French digs at Arcy-sur-Cure and La Ferrassie or the 400,000-year-old scratches on an elephant rib from the Thuringian site Bilzingsleben, which have no clear function but are aesthetically appealing, are often interpreted as evidence of their creators' ritual attitudes. They bring up the question of when art had its beginning. Was it already the Neanderthal who began to portray his environment and himself in art? Or was Cro-Magnon Man, the modern human, the first who released his creative potential along the path of cave painting and the invention of musical instruments like the 30,000-year-old bone flute from Geissenklösterle? Are the scratches perhaps only signs of work, so that the elephant rib from Bilzingsleben was perhaps simply a work stand? Often, assertions that objects have a symbolic character seem to be based more on wishful thinking than on carefully thought-out and evidentially supported hypotheses. Nevertheless, objects repeatedly turn up even from the Lower Paleolithic Era (more than 200,000 years ago) that cannot be regarded simply as the result of simple tool working. Eye-catching materials such as lead, especially beautifully-formed stones, or a fossil sea urchin, found in the northern French cave of Merry-sur-Yonne, were apparently purposely collected and some-times transported long distances—perhaps expressing an early-developed aesthetic sensitivity.

The oldest Neanderthal jewelry pieces come from the period 35,000 to c. 115,000 years BP. Among the extremely rare finds of this sort belong a partially drilled-through fox tooth from La Quina in the Charente (France). Other finds include a bored wolf tail vertebra from Bocksteinschmiede in the Lone Valley in Baden-Württemberg and a wolf tooth from Repolust Cave in Austria. Possible Neanderthal jewelry items also come from the French find site Grotte du Renne in Arcy-sur-Cure (Figure 17). These finds of bone and tooth remains, at 36 sites in all, can perhaps be valued as the crown jewels in the search for the Neanderthals' jewelry and artistic ability. The objects, with holes drilled in them and provided with grooves, were unearthed together with stone tools of the Chatelperronian, a tool

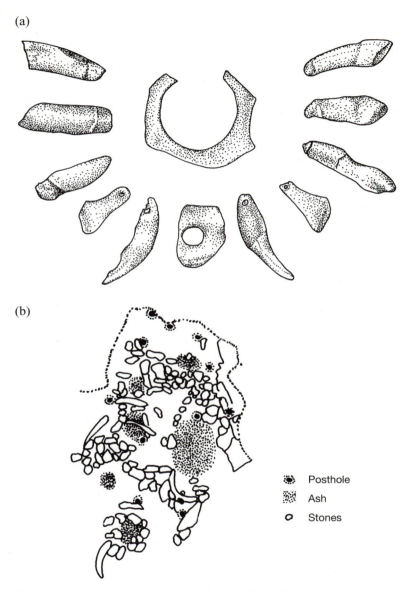

Figure 17 (a) Ice-age jewelry from Burgundy: this bone jewelry was uncovered at the French Neanderthal find site Arcy-sur-Cure. The necklace has an estimated age of 40,000–35,000 years. (b) Campsite of Arcy-sur-Cure.

epoch that, as already mentioned, was for a long time attributed only to modern humans. After the discovery of part of a neanderthaloid skull, it is obvious that Neanderthals too displayed corresponding artistic ability and skill—if the jewelry really comes from the same find level.

Color pigments like red ochre or black manganese oxide also suggest possible ritual or artistic behavior. It is unclear how and why the Neanderthals used nature's palette—perhaps it was to paint their bodies or dye clothes. Another possibility is that they used natural colors to impregnate skins, which would certainly indicate that the Neanderthals had very highly developed technical abilities.

BURIAL CUSTOM OR CULT OF THE DEAD?

Speculation runs rampant when it comes to prehistoric ritual behavior. The dead of the ice age provide the most conclusive evidence for the existence of rituals. For the first time in human history, burials took place. They can possibly be interpreted as evidence for solicitude, love of neighbor, and culturally developed manners of the individuals of a group toward one another. This perspective was, to be sure, not accepted without question in the early twentieth century. Many scholars of the time were of the opinion that such burials were, by our standards, not carried out intentionally. The burial of a human being also presumes that those left behind grieve, and in their sorrow honor the deceased. That, at least, is our average experience of the procedure. But perhaps the dead were also buried "only" for purely pragmatic reasons, that is, to clear away the decaying corpse, if possible without odor and hygienically, and thus not attract animals. For whatever reason the Neanderthals carried out burials, some motive must have moved the Neanderthals in *all* regions of Europe to dispose of their dead under the earth.

For paleoanthropology and archaeology, the fact that burials were conducted is highly significant, because without burials the mortal remains of our more or less related forebears would have been left exposed to the destructive action of weather and animals. Most of the 35 Neanderthal skeleton finds that suggest purposeful burial that have been uncovered to date come from caves and the area of cliff overhangs, in other words in naturally protected locations that the Neanderthals visited repeatedly. Flat, up to one-meter deep graves were dug to bury the dead. The deceased was mostly laid in the grave on his back or crouching—lying on one side with drawn-up legs. Grave deposits, such as the mountain goat horns in the case of the boy from Teshik Tash in Uzbekistan, are rather rare. Graves from the Upper Paleolithic (40,000–11,500 years BP) are richer in grave deposits. Jewelry-adorned dead like the ice-age man from Sungir with pearl-embroidered clothing mentioned above (Figure 20) are found much more frequently among modern humans than with Neanderthals. In the 1970s, people did not want to accept this fact. In the period of general hippie bliss and Woodstock exuberance, the view came about—when the supposed "flower tomb" of Shanidar in northern Iraq had been uncovered—that as early as the Neanderthals people had buried their dead with flowers. As discussed above, analysis of the surrounding sediment has, since that time, showed that the fossil flower pollen was really the remains of food "smuggled in" subsequently by voles. There was also no trace of fossil "flower power" in the Neanderthal graves of Le Moustier, La Quina, Saint Césaire, Spy, Amud, Tabun, or Kiik Koba in the Crimea. Nonetheless, stone implements, animal bones, and animal teeth were discovered within graves in these places, although they may well be objects of general daily life that were only included in the grave coincidentally.

Pigment remains of red ochre have been identified in the graves near La Ferrassie, Spy, and La Chapelle-aux-Saints. But it is not known what significance colors had in Neanderthal burials, or what cultic practices might lie behind the use of natural pigments.

The isolated finds of Neanderthal skulls have also given rise to speculation. "Headless" skeleton remains like the c. 60,000-year-old bones of a young man in Kebara have led to the supposition that the ice-age Europeans separated the skulls of the dead and when possible buried them in different places from the body, in order to remember their dead there. At all events, no evidence whatsoever of any grave plundering was discovered in the case of the Kebara skeleton (Figure 14). The skull therefore must have been painstakingly removed after the body was reduced to a skeleton and taken out of the grave, because the right wisdom tooth provides evidence that the skull too was buried there at some point. Multi-stage burials of the dead are by no means rare in human history, so this case is not evidence of a unique "Neanderthal cult" but rather of a widely disseminated interaction of the living with the dead of their group.

Discussion of the question as to whether Neanderthals were cannibals has rarely been dispassionate or free of bias. It is not scientifically sound to link or indeed equate every stripping of the flesh from a corpse with cannibalism. Thus the cut marks on the world-famous Neanderthal from Mettmann, but also on his distant neighbors from Marillac, Combe Grenal, Teshik Tash, and Ochtendung, are apparently the result of skinning and stripping the flesh, but are not proof of cannibalism. We know of the symbolic consumption of the dead in many archaic cultures as a symbolic transferal of the dead person's former strength to the living who remain behind. But this practice too should be distinguished from cannibalism. The differentiation becomes still more difficult in the case of the finds from Krapina in Croatia. Traces of fire, cuts, and blows have been found on the fossils of more than 24 individuals discovered there, suggesting the external use of force in the breaking of bones and skulls. Apparently the Neanderthals there dined on the marrow of their dead—if this is so, how often this took place in a ritual context can no longer be reconstructed. A completely different picture emerges from Moula-Guercy, a Neanderthal find site in southeastern France. Here, the state of the find speaks unambiguously for cannibalism. In the midst of goat and red deer food remains that the Neanderthals left behind, investigators found human bones that displayed open marrow cavities as well as traces of cuts and scrapes. Microscopic examination of the finds also shows that humans were apparently prepared before being eaten. Their cadavers were prepared, at least so it appears, no differently from those of the animals whose remains lie round about.

Thus Neanderthals clearly interacted with the dead of their species in widely varying fashions, ranging from painstaking burial, eventually taking place in stages, through symbolic consumption of parts of the body, to apparent cannibalism. In this respect, each find must be treated independently and be carefully interpreted. Bias regarding the Neanderthals and the attempt to set them off from modern humans as brutish and animal-like leads to error, as the interpretation of the isolated skull from Monte Circeo has shown: it was not caused by the Neanderthals' cannibalistic customs, but was the result of hyenas feeding.

THE NEANDERTHALS' SOCIAL BEHAVIOR

One of the most important research findings for answering the question of how "human" the Neanderthals were can be seen in the fact that 40 percent of the burial finds are of children and adolescents. From this we may conclude that both young and old, who were cared for until death, were just as important in the social structure of our ice-age fellow humans as the fully productive adult Neanderthals were. How Neanderthals divided up the necessary tasks—whether the men hunted, the old taught, the women gathered and cooked, and the children played and minced food for the elderly—appears to be the realm of fantasy. Such reconstructions reflect the speculative abilities of today's *Homo sapiens*, who first developed as African neighbors of the Neanderthal and later, after their emigration to the Levant, shared their habitat with the Neanderthals for 40,000 to 60,000 years. It is impossible to say how much further interface existed between the life of the modern emigrant from Africa and the native European Neanderthals. There are too few finds that give evidence of close proximity as neighbors—in the sense of next-door neighbors living side by side. Still, a relatively peaceful coexistence can be presumed, along with the mutual use of available resources in a radius of several hundred kilometers.

There is no trace of warlike conflict, as has ofen been propagated in the past in the genre of so-called "paleofiction" or in popular magazines. How human or inhuman the Neanderthal might have been from the perspective of the modern, surviving human species, whether he could sing or not, whether he had a complex language or only made sounds, whether he shared food or was solitary in his struggle—we can only be certain that the Neanderthals were the last limb of a very successful human line in evolutionary history. They successfully confronted the environmental conditions of the ice age with strategies and techniques, and managed to get along in their environment. They were not, however, particularly creative in our modern sense. Europe's cultural and creative revolution began only toward the end of the Neanderthal era, about 45,000 years ago. The tool, which had remained fundamentally unchanged for many generations, began at that time to display significant changes from century to century. A dramatically rapid cultural development dawned in the last phase of the Paleolithic Era. For the first time, there is evidence in human history of art, which presupposes a greater manual dexterity, a high order of abstract thought, and aesthetic sensitivity. Works appeared like the 32,000-year-old lionman statue from Vogelherd Cave in Swabia, mammoth-ivory pendants in the shape of horses from the Russian Sungir, flutes and cave paintings. This was the same period during which the last Neanderthals were probably troubled about the preservation of their population. Beginning 27,000 years ago, our form of the human species lived alone on the planet earth—a state of affairs that had never before existed since the evolution of humankind, with one fascinating exception discovered recently in Southeast Asia (see Chapter 6).

6

ENCOUNTERS WITH
THE MODERN

EVE CAME FROM AFRICA

The Neanderthal. A German world star, a European "special model" of evolution, who, ever since the mid-nineteenth century, has given the science of paleoanthropology enough fossil fodder to research the origin of the human family. One who, after decades of false valuation as the dumb brute of the stone age, has been transformed into the clever hunter. It has taken a long time for the Neanderthals to become the best-researched archaic humans. That they have taught present-day humankind that there used to be other sorts of humans than those of the present appears revolutionary enough in itself. That the find that gave them their name still produces headlines 150 years after its discovery in the Neander Valley is astonishing, dealing as it does "only" with old bones. But these very old bones unlocked a secret in 1997, using the most modern technology, that for the first time ended the long debate about the relationship between *Homo sapiens* and *Homo neanderthalensis*: Neanderthals are not our ancestors. These, one and all, originated in Africa—whether pre-human, primitive human, early human, or modern human (Figure 18). We all have genetic material in our mortal remains that can still provide evidence after our death that we are descended from the family of the African primal Eve and the African primal Adam.

While the Neanderthals were developing in Europe, the modern humans, or at least their ancestors, emerged in Africa about 200,000 to 500,000 years ago. The oldest representative of our modern primal family discovered to date is the c. 160,000-year-old Herto Man (Figure 19), whose skull was found in Ethiopia's Afar Depression along with two other modern humans. More fossils of our early modern forebears come from South Africa. The finds at Klasies River Mouth and Border Cave produced ages of 100,000 and 150,000 years. Another modern human skeleton, recently dated to 210,000 years BP, comes from the Kibish Formation in

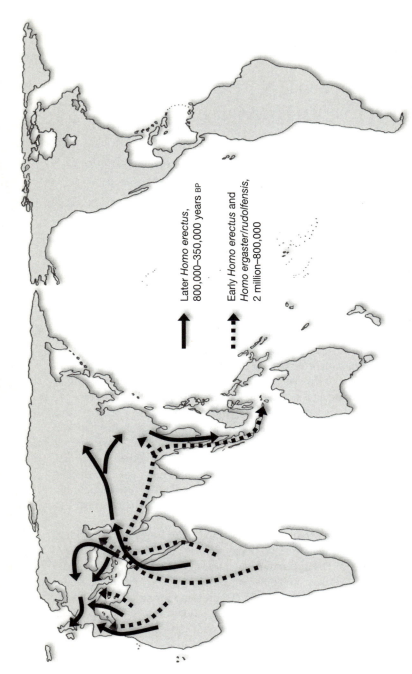

Later *Homo erectus*,
800,000–350,000 years BP

Early *Homo erectus* and
Homo ergaster/rudolfensis,
2 million–800,000

Figure 18 Two main phases of emigration from Africa can be demonstrated for *Homo erectus* (about 2 million years ago, and about 800,000 years ago) (above). Modern humans (*Homo sapiens*) left Africa in several phases beginning about 120,000 years ago (opposite).

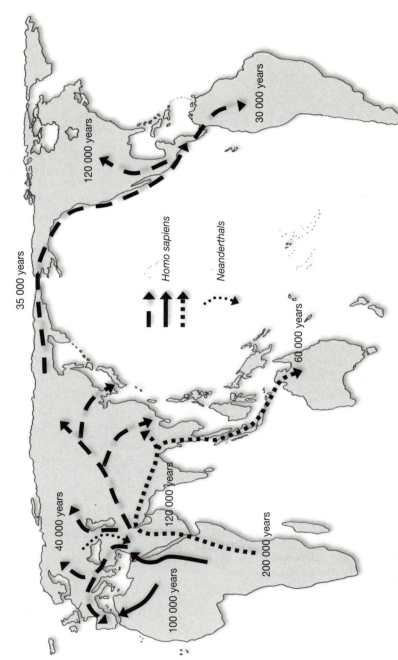

Figure 18 Continued

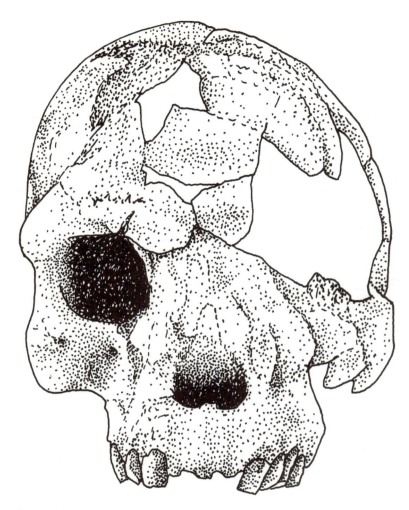

Figure 19 *Homo sapiens* came from Africa: the Herto skull, with an age of
160,000 years, is the oldest remains of a modern human yet found.
The skull, uncovered in the Afar region of Ethiopia in 2003, supports
the "Out of Africa" hypothesis in the debate about the origin of
modern humans.

the Omo Basin of southern Ethiopia. Early archaic *Homo sapiens* types, represented by the skull from Bodo (Ethiopia), the skull from Lake Ndutu west of Olduvai Gorge (Tanzania), the Kabwe skull (Zambia), and the finds from Salé (Morocco) and Eyasi (Tanzania) have been established within a chronological level of 200,000 to 500,000 years. Further transitional forms from the period 100,000–200,000 years BP have been found at the South African Florisbad, Eliye Springs (Kenya), Laetoli (Tanzania), and Jebel Irhoud in Morocco.

The fossil bones of modern humans from Africa tell an unmistakable tale, thanks to the location of the finds: at the latest about 160,000 years ago the first modern humans emerged in Africa, but by 120,000 years ago they could be found in the Near East in the Levant (Figure 18). The fossils from Qafzeh near Nazareth in northern Israel and Skhul near Haifa, whose age has been fixed at 100,000–120,000 or 80,000–100,000 years by radio-carbon dating, are the oldest evidence yet discovered of modern humans' emigration from Africa. Both the African and the Israelite finds support a theory known as the "Out of Africa" hypothesis. Viewed geographically, according to this theory Africa is the origination point of anatomically modern humans. From Africa they spread out and settled the entire world. How much they associated with other human types like the Neanderthals in the process, whether they displaced them or simply lived with them, is among the many speculations that have been aired again and again in past years. Against the purely African origin model is the multiregional hypothesis, which argues that modern humans originated on different continents—in Asia, Europe, and Africa—from regional ancestors. In this model, interbreeding with Neanderthals also entered the picture as a possible source of the Europeans. Likewise, discussions about the development of Cro-Magnon Man (the oldest discovered European) and the Neanderthal as a possible ancestor have fanned the quarrel between the proponents of the two theories. But neither of the two hypotheses offered a satisfying answer to the question of whether modern humans supplanted, replaced, or assimilated the now-extinct Neanderthals, or indeed if the Neanderthals were our direct ancestors.

MODERN HUMANS' GENETIC CODE

The Neanderthals can be attested in the Near East just like the oldest modern humans outside of Africa. Modern humans might thus perhaps have been their neighbors, with whom they co-existed for more than 60,000 years, at least in the Levant. Which of the two human groups was there first—the Neanderthals from the north or the modern humans from the south—remains unclear for the present, but is not important in answering the question about the origin of *Homo sapiens* anyway. Light broke into the darkness of the two opposing theories in research results published in 1987 of mitochondrial DNA (mtDNA). This research has now been established as the "Black Eve" theory and has entered the history of paleogenetics. To give a brief summary, researchers demonstrated that the mitochondrial DNA of African women has the most variants and is therefore the oldest population of humans alive today. Mitochondrial DNA is only passed on through the mother's side, since a female egg cell is a complete cell, which contains tiny "power plants"—mitochondria— besides the cell nucleus, while the male seed only receives the cell nucleus in fusion. As the inherited material duplicates, mutations always appear, which have a larger impact on the mitochondria than they do on the cell nucleus. In the mtDNA there are thus demonstrably more mutations than in the cell nucleus DNA. For this reason, the female mtDNA is better suited to look for and determine differences, in order to make comparisons between nearly identical organisms, such as human beings.

As a result, mtDNA functions as a sort of molecular clock. The number of variations that can be established in the mtDNA of different people allows scientists to draw conclusions about the length of time that has passed since the permutation appeared. The examination of Australians, Europeans, Asians, and all other populations of humans living today has proven that they could have divided phylogenetically from each other only a short time ago. If one traces the mutation process back, it can be concluded that a primal "Eve" must have lived in Africa about 200,000 years ago. In family trees that were made to outline the mtDNA sequences, the African variants lie closest to the origin, which means that they display the most differences that can be established in the current world population; they certainly formed the pool of variants that all modern humans "tap."

The ancestress of all modern humans thus lived on the dark continent— so it makes sense to look for the primal father in Africa, too. The Y-chromosome is a region in the genome that offers the male counterpart to mtDNA; it is passed on exclusively from father to son. It is no surprise after the study outlined above to learn that studies of male genes have established that the primal Adam also came from Africa. With these two conclusions it is settled: the modern human originated in Africa and emigrated thence to the entire world, although possibly in several expansion phases (Figure 18).

But what does this mean for Neanderthal research? Not much at first glance, since the confirmation or rejection of the two theories through DNA analysis only goes to answer the question of where anatomically modern humans originated. But could DNA analysis be equally helpful in the question of possible interbreeding between modern humans and Neanderthals? That is one of the most-asked questions in paleoanthropology. The close proximity of find sites of modern humans (Skhul, Qafzeh, Figure 13c and Figure 23 in the Appendix) and Neanderthals (Kebara, Tabun) in Israel attest that the two hominid groups lived near each other without problems for at least 60,000 years. Such a long co-existence in the same region leads to the question of whether they might have met or even interbred. Traces of such possible interchanges would then be evident anatomically, if one recalls that the sturdy Neanderthal braved the ice age and the more lightly built *Homo sapiens* had fled the African sun. But all skull and skeleton parts that have been discovered have been—even though after some errors and confusion—classified either as clearly modern or clearly neandertholoid. It was only the discovery of the so-called "hybrid child" in 1998 at Lagar Velho in Portugal (Figure 20a) that gave new impetus to proponents of the interbreeding theory.

The nearly complete skeleton of a child about four years old, estimated at a geological age of c. 25,000 years, lay in a bed of burned pine twigs and was covered with red ochre—a typical modern human burial style (Figure 20a). Most of the anatomical characteristics also attest that this must have been a child of modern humankind. But a closer look reveals certain anomalous features that are more like those of a Neanderthal child. The receding lower jaw, the attachment points of the chest muscles, and the short, strong tibias suggest a hybrid population that lay between anatomically modern and Neanderthal humans. The find created a sensation in both the scholarly and the popular press for a long time. The Lagar Velho child suggests that modern humans indeed originated in Africa but would have interbred with the pre-existing archaic human types in other regions. But this thesis is not supported by the results of a study that Fred Spoor conducted of the Lagar Velho child's inner ear. He has proven that the position of the semicircular canals of the labyrinth in the child's inner ear is that of a modern human, not a Neanderthal. Whatever family affiliation is established for the supposed hybrid child with the help of new research methods, the result remains that local, sporadic interbreeding between human species like the Neanderthals and anatomically modern humans was not unlikely. Such a process would have repeatedly mixed the gene pools of the two populations. But then shouldn't we find traces of Neanderthal DNA in our genes? This is a question that can only be answered by the extraction of fossil DNA.

Today, the methods of paleogenetics permit time travel to the deepest depths of the genes of extinct organisms and living creatures whose DNA has survived in favorable environmental conditions, such as buried in ice

.)

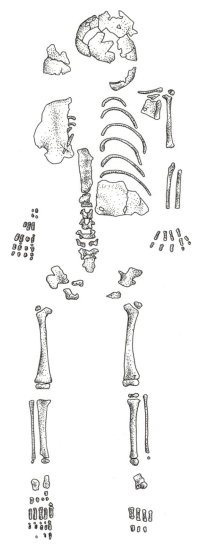

Figure 20 Burial rituals improve the probability of finding nearly complete human fossils. (a) The supposed hybrid child from Lagar Velho (Portugal) was laid to rest about 24,500 years ago, and excavated in 1998. (b) The approximately 60-year-old man from Sungir, Russia, was buried about 28,000 years ago with rich accessories consisting of 2936 individual pearls. Magnificent burials such as these can first be found with modern humans, not the Neanderthals.

(b)

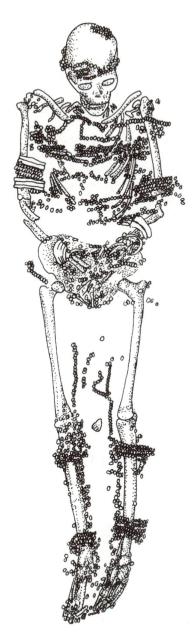

Figure 20 Continued

or in anaerobic bogs. The first study of the DNA sequence of a fossil human took place in 1997. The DNA came from the original Neanderthal from the Neander Valley. This 40,000-year-old fossil was granted the posthumous honor of donating a piece of its humerus for molecular study by Svante Pääbo, Matthias Krings, and Ralf W. Schmitz, the rediscoverers of the site of the Neanderthal's original discovery. It was possible to take mitochondrial DNA from the 3.5-gram sample, which was combined in a strand 379 base pairs long. A comparison of the fossil Neanderthal DNA with the DNA of humans living today showed an average of 27 divergences. That is a lot, since the sequences of a modern human show differences of only eight base pairs on average. What does this mean for the relationship between *Homo sapiens* and *Homo neanderthalensis*? The molecular biology periodical *Cell* declared on the significance of the study unequivocally: "Neanderthals were not our ancestors." Thus it appeared that the relationship between us modern humans and the archaic European from the Neander Valley had been made plain once and for all. But there was also some doubt about the published result. For one thing, impurities can always enter DNA samples; thus for example the DNA of the Neanderthal researcher Fuhlrott could have been mixed in the sample through a tiny hair. However, those in charge describe the sample as pure. The result might also have been different if the researches had used cell nucleus DNA, because nuclear DNA stores different information than mitochondrial DNA. But all of this is speculation. It is clear, on the basis of this epoch-making study, that the last common ancestor of Neanderthals and modern humans must have lived about 500,000 years ago and that the last Neanderthals made no decisive contribution to the gene pool of humans alive today.

THE NEANDERTHALS' DEPARTURE

Although this result might have been crushing for many "Neanderthal fans," the achievement of Pääbo, Krings, and Schmitz cannot be overstated. We can eagerly anticipate further new interpretations, made possible through modern research techniques, which will continue to revolutionize paleoanthropology. These new methods include computer tomography and the study of isotopes, which permit conclusions about the morphology and diet of our forebears. The Zürich scientists Christoph Zollikofer and Marcia Ponce de Léon have shown themselves to be masters at the virtual reconstruction of human fossils by means of tomography and computer graphics. Without having to handle a fossil, the appearance of fossil humans like the Neanderthals can be recreated using rotating computer graphics. Parts of a fossil can be mirrored and inserted where the counterpart is missing, so that a complete picture of the organism can emerge. By means of stereolithography, plastic models can be prepared based on this foundation, which then serve reconstructors as the basis to make the most exact possible models of the soft tissues and features of the former living creature.

In the future, the TNT Project (www.The-Neanderthal-Tools.org) will provide access to this and other data. The internet platform offers laypeople and scientists alike access to data on the 300 Neanderthals found to date and their 130 find sites—an ambitious project that will also promote scientific democracy. For the first time, scientists from all over the world will be able to subject fossils to careful scrutiny that up to now have been largely inaccessible. The scientists' already limited travel budget will be spared, and an active exchange of data about fossils will be possible. Measurements of skulls, jaws, and bones can be undertaken on the internet as if directly.

All of these new processes, projects, and research methods place scholars in the fortunate position of being able to evaluate the old Neanderthals in ever new ways and perhaps to answer some of the unanswered questions about them. But whatever the method, paleo-anthropologists must always emphasize the significance of new fossil finds. Every new find represents a significant scholarly achievement in itself. Even Ralf W. Schmitz and Jürgen Thissen's rediscovery of the lost original find site of the Neanderthal in the Neander Valley and unearthing of new bone fragments of the skeleton appears as a small scientific miracle. One hundred and fifty years after Fuhlrott's description of the Neanderthal's discovery, today the additional find pieces have given the man from Mettmann a new face (Figure 1).

The chronology and find map of the last Neanderthals in Europe have also received a new face thanks to recent discoveries. For a long time it was assumed that the appearance of modern humans was accompanied by a pushing out of the Neanderthals into inhospitable, unfruitful regions such as the Iberian Peninsula. New finds could support this "ghetto" hypothesis. The Neanderthal fossils from Zafarraya in Spain are dated to an age of 28,000–32,000 years BP. Since there had been no later finds, it was assumed that, as the last Neanderthals, they lived in a sort of ghetto situation, until their population could no longer maintain itself. However, Vindija, a cave find site in northwestern Croatia, shows that during the same period there were still Neanderthal populations in other locations. The "youngest Neanderthals" found there, with an age of 28,000 years, lived in one of the most fruitful regions of central Europe—so the theory that they were forced out appears to have been thoroughly disproven. The stone tools discovered there, from the Mousterian and the Aurignacian (hitherto ascribed only to modern humans), also suggest that there was a peaceful interaction between Neanderthals and modern humans, which perhaps included even tool exchange—so the evidence does not support a forcible driving out and ghettoization.

Meanwhile, the picture of the Pleistocene interaction between modern humans and Neanderthals has been presented to the public as less peaceful. Thus as recently as spring 2000 a German news magazine published an article entitled "The War of the First Humans—How *Homo sapiens* Drove Out the Neanderthal." The entire title page was festooned with an illustration of two battle-maddened Europeans, a Neanderthal with eye ridges and brown eyes on the left and the modern human with long nose and blue eyes on the right. The *Homo sapiens* was presented as warlord and successful conqueror, who contended with the "rival" Neanderthals in a struggle for the better land, the better woman, and the better animals. Popular scientific literature often speaks of the "success model" *Homo sapiens* and of how he started his "triumphant progress" in the new world, becoming a creative sculptor and superior hunter. The "fate" of the Neanderthals is then for the most part described sadly, with frequent mentions of the "departure model" Neanderthal. With all of these platitudes, which rest on antiquated stereotypes of the stupid, inferior Neanderthal brute in contrast to the intelligent modern Herculean figures from Africa, the simple explanation for the disappearance of an entire species is not considered at all: like every other species in the animal kingdom, including humans, the Neanderthals had to produce enough offspring to maintain their population. Perhaps, though, the improved hunting weapons of *Homo sapiens* could also have been a reason why the latter species survived to the present day. Bloodthirsty speculations feed the desire for an image of a rivalry between *Homo sapiens* and *Homo neanderthalensis* that attracts readers and appeals to the martial spirit of our present age, but are of no use to science. If one sticks to the facts, it is clear that, even if we only consider the light population density of Europe, any sort of "war" between modern humans and Neanderthals would hardly have been possible.

The scenario according to which the Neanderthals were swept away by some insidious malady appears just as far from reality. Such an epidemic would have to have left behind concrete signs, but not a trace has been discovered so far. The Neanderthals were also well established in Europe's changing warm and cold climate in the ice age. Since in the period between 50,000 and 30,000 years BP there is evidence of a total of 18 climate changes that took place, the exit of the Neanderthals because of some sort of climatic catastrophe seems unlikely. So, what plausible explanation remains for the disappearance of the Neanderthals, a thoroughly successful human species? The theory that the Neanderthals died out due to a reproduction failure appears most probable. So-called "bottle-neck" situations, points of population restriction, are not unusual in human history and could thus also have affected the Neanderthals. In evolution, the extinction of a species is just as normal as the appearance of a new one.

What precisely led to the Neanderthals' disappearance can thus not be explained here. The only point that is certain is that there is no more evidence for Neanderthal existence after about 27,000 years BP. The last traces of this species have been found in the caves near Zafarraya in Spain and Vindija in Croatia that were mentioned above. More fossil remains of the last Neanderthals are the 31,000-year-old bones from Figueira Brava in Portugal, as well as the finds from Arcy-sur-Care and Saint Césaire in France. Between 40,000 and 30,000 years BP, the Mousterian tool culture was already practically obsolete, and the finer Aurignacian had made its entry into *Homo sapiens'* stoneworking shops. At the same time as the "invention" of this technique, a cultural revolution took place that, as already mentioned, gave rise to the first figural art in the form of the lionman statue from the Swabian Hohlenstein-Stadel Cave or the horse carving from the Vogelherd Cave (Figure 21) or musical instruments like the bone flute from Geissenklösterle. But we can only speculate about how much this technological and creative wave also changed the Neanderthals' world.

For us "survivors," it is nonetheless important to recognize that we as *Homo sapiens* were not unique. Until 27,000 years ago we shared our territory in Europe with another human species, the Neanderthals. In southeast Asia, *Homo sapiens* even lived another 9000 years alongside another human species, *Homo floresiensis* (Figure 22). This totally unexpected species, discovered in 2004, has, like the Neanderthal, a different anatomy from the modern human. The dwarfish "hobbit" of Flores displays, with a volume of only 380 cm^3, the smallest brain of all hominids in the human family "bush" found to date. Probably he was a descendent of very early African emigrants, who left Africa even before the *Homo erectus*, perhaps more than two million years ago. The find did not merely raise the spirits of its Australian discoverer. With the demonstrated existence of a new human species, the debate over the origins of the human family—between the "Out of Africa" theorists and the multiregionalists—flared up again. In any case, the fossils from Flores attest that human evolution can only really be understood when we pay attention not just to the anatomical and chronological classification of the finds, but above all to their geographical distribution too.

On different continents at different times, different developments took place that produced different human types more than once—like the

(a)

(b)

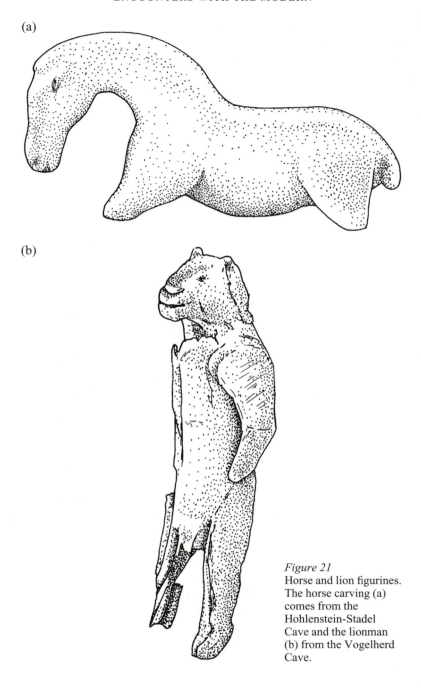

Figure 21
Horse and lion figurines.
The horse carving (a)
comes from the
Hohlenstein-Stadel
Cave and the lionman
(b) from the Vogelherd
Cave.

Neanderthals in Europe and the dwarf people of the island of Flores. We, *Homo sapiens*, are the remnant of all these regional developments—generalists, who increasingly specialized, invented agriculture, autos, and atom bombs, and populated the whole earth. *Homo sapiens* is a historian who has the ability to seek, discover, and interpret the evidence of his forebears and to share these findings with his fellow humans. As the last remaining human species, it is we who present the history and the image of the Neanderthals to the public. Today, 150 years after the discovery of the first fossil human bones to be identified as the remains of a Neanderthal,

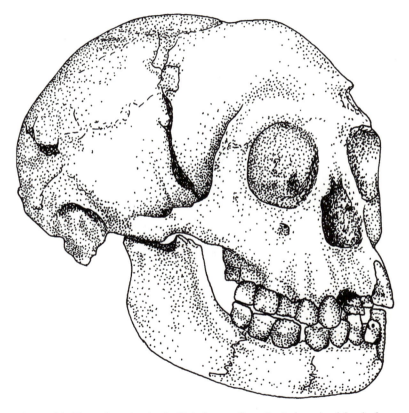

Figure 22 *Homo floresiensis*, the little human from the Indonesian island of Flores, attracted worldwide media interest. Long after the last Neanderthal, the c. 18,000-year-old "dwarf" is further evidence that, beside the human group to which we belong, other types of humans existed. It is very likely that *Homo floresiensis* comes from a very old branching off from the earliest emigrants from Africa.

we now know that the first Europeans have a long, exciting, and successful life story to tell. Neanderthals existed far longer than we have thus far, and therefore should receive from us a fitting place in the evolutionary model of becoming human. For we have not yet proven that we will be able to deal with the demands of our world longer and more successfully than our extinct fellow humans did.

APPENDIX

IMPORTANT FOSSIL SITES OF THE EARLY EUROPEANS

Early Homo erectus (1.8 million–800,000 years BP):
Dmanisi (Georgia) (Figure 6), Orçe (Spain), Ceprano (Italy)

European Homo erectus (Homo heidelbergensis) (800,000–350,000 years BP):
Atapuerca (Gran Dolina), (Spain); Mauer (Figure 9), Bilzingsleben (Germany) (Figure 10); Arago (France) (Figure 9); Boxgrove (England); Petralona (Figure 9), Apidima (Greece)

Ante-Neanderthals (Homo steinheimensis) in Europe (c. 350,000–180,000 years BP):
Steinheim (Germany) (Figure 12), Swanscombe (England), Vértesszöllös (Hungary), Atapuerca (Sima de los Huesos) (Spain) (Figure 12), Pontnewydd (Wales)

Early Neanderthals in Europe (c. 180,000–90,000 years BP):
Wimar-Ehringsdorf (Germany), Krapina (Croatia) (Figure 12), Saccopastore (Italy), Forbes Quarry (Gibraltar) (Figure 2), Altamura (Italy), Ochtendung (Germany)

Classic Neanderthals in Europe and the Near East (Homo neanderthalensis) (c. 90,000–27,000 years BP):
Neandertal (Figure 1), Salzgitter-Lebenstedt (Germany); La Chapelle-aux-Saints (Figure 13), La Ferrasie, La Quina, Le Moustier, St Césaire, Arcy sur Cure (Figure 17), Arc (France); Engis (Figure 2), La Naulette, Spy (Belgium); Monte Circeo (Italy); Shanidar (Kurdistan) (Figure 13); Kebara (Israel) (Figure 14); Teshik Tash (Uzbekistan); Subalyuk (Hungary); Dederiyeh (Syria)

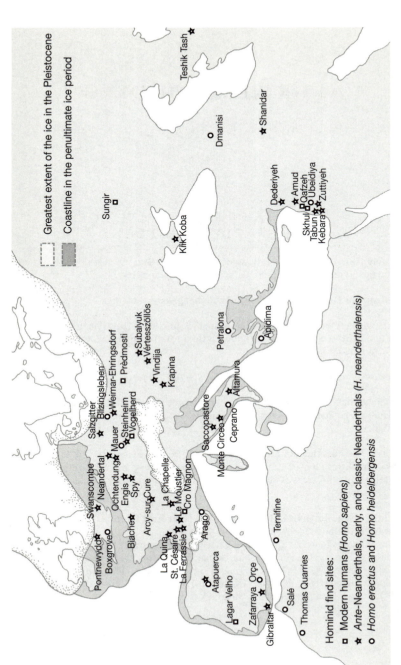

Figure 23 The location of important finds of early Europeans.

FURTHER READING

SURVEYS

Conard, N.J. (ed.) (2004) *Woher kommt der Mensch?* Tübingen: Attempto.

Foley, R. (2000) *Menschen vor* Homo sapiens. *Wie und warum sich unsere Art durchsetzte.* Stuttgart: Thorbecke.

Henke, W. and Rothe, H. (2000) *Stammesgeschichte des Menschen. Eine Einführung.* Berlin & Heidelberg: Springer Verlag (standard work).

Klein, R.G. (1989) *The Human Career: Human Biological and Cultural Origins.* Chicago: University of Chicago Press.

Kuckenburg, M. (1999) *Lag Eden im Neandertal? Auf der Suche nach dem frühen Menschen.* Munich: Econ (goldmine for quotations).

Leakey, R.E. (1994) *The Origin of Humankind.* New York: Basic Books.

Lewin, R. (1987) *Bones of Contention: Controversies in the Search for Human Origins.* New York: Simon and Schuster.

Schrenk, F. (2003) *Die Frühzeit des Menschen.* Munich: C.H. Beck.

Schrenk, F. and Bromage, T.G. (2000) *Adams Eltern—Expeditionen in die Welt der Frühmenschen.* Munich: C.H. Beck.

Tattersall, I. (1995) *The Fossil Trail: How We Know What We Think We Know about Human Evolution.* Oxford: Oxford University Press.

HOMO ERECTUS AND *HOMO HEIDELBERGENSIS*

Jia, L. and Huang, W. (1990) *The Story of Peking Man.* Beijing: Foreign Languages Press.

Leakey, R.E. and Walker, A.C. (1985) *Homo erectus* unearthed, *National Geographic* 168(5): 624–629.

Wagner, G.A. and Beinhauer, G. (eds) (1997) Homo heidelbergensis *von Mauer: Das Auftreten des Menschen in Europa.* Heidelberg: HVA.

NEANDERTHALS AND *HOMO SAPIENS*

Auffermann, B. and Orschiedt, J. (2002) *Die Neandertaler. Eine Spurensuche.* Stuttgart: Theiss (a synthetic overview).

Cavalli-Sforza, L.L. (2000) *Genes, Peoples, and Languages.* New York: North Point Press.

Henke, W., Kieser, N. and Schnaubelt, W. (1996) *Die Neandertalerin. Botschafterin der Vorzeit.* Gelsenkirchen: Edition Archaea (reconstructions of Neanderthals).

Schmitz, R.W. and Thissen, J. (2002) *Neandertal. Die Geschichte geht weiter.* Heidelberg: Spektrum Akademischer Verlag (rediscovery of the fossil site from 1856).

Stringer, C. and Gamble, C. (1994) *In Search of the Neanderthals.* London: Thames & Hudson.

Tattersall, I. (1999) *Neandertaler. Der Streit um unsere Ahnen.* Basel: Birkhäuser.

Trinkaus, E. and Shipman, P. (1993) *The Neanderthals: Changing the Image of Mankind.* New York: Knopf.

INDEX

Related titles from Routledge

Archaeology
The Basics

Second Edition

Clive Gamble

'Gamble's book provides an excellent introduction to the aims and
methods of archaeology, which is by no means easy within the confines
of one book. But to do so in a manner which is intellectually engaged
with the subject matter and which evokes the excitement and interest
of archaeological work is a considerable achievement. The best short
introduction to the subject I know and one which will become a standard
text for any teacher of archaeology or related subject.' – *Chris Gosden,
Pitt Rivers Museum, University of Oxford, UK*

'The digger boasting the worn stub of a trowel in their right back trouser
pocket should feel incomplete without a copy of *Archaeology: The
Basics* in the other.' – *Current Archaeology*

This second edition from our successful Basics series presents another
chance to delve into this increasingly popular subject. Fully updated,
Archaeology: The Basics has also been revised to reflect growth in areas
such as material culture, human evolution and the political use of the past.
Lively and engaging, some of the key questions answered include:

*   What are the basic concepts of archaeology?
*   How and what do we know about people and objects from the past?
*   What makes a good explanation in archaeology?
*   How do we know where to look?

From everyday examples to the more obscure, this is essential reading for
all students, independent archaeologists and indeed all those who want to
know more about archaeological thought, history and practice. A piece of
broken pottery will never seem the same again.

Hb: 978–0–415–35974–0
Pb: 978–0–415–35975–7

Related titles from Routledge

Archaeology: An Introduction

Fourth Edition

Kevin Greene

'The best one-stop introduction to archaeology.'
Mick Aston, University of Bristol, Time Team

This substantially updated fourth edition of the highly popular, and comprehensive *Archaeology: An Introduction* is aimed at all beginners in the subject. In a lucid and accessible style Kevin Greene takes the reader on a journey which covers history, techniques and the latest theories. He explains the discovery and excavation of sites, outlines major dating methods, gives clear explanations of scientific techniques, and examines current theories and controversies.

This fourth edition constitutes the most extensive reshaping of the text to date. New features include:

- A completely new user-friendly text design with initial chapter overviews and final conclusions, key references for each chapter section, an annotated guide to further reading, a glossary, refreshed illustrations, case studies and examples, bibliography and full index
- A new companion website built for this edition providing hyperlinks from contents list to individual chapter summaries which in turn link to key websites and other material
- An important new chapter on current theory emphasizing the richness of sources of analogy or interpretation available today.

Archaeology: An Introduction will interest students and teachers at pre-university and undergraduate level as well as enthusiastic general readers of archaeology. The stimulating coverage of the history, methods, science and theory of archaeology make this a book which has a life both within and beyond the academy.

Hb: 978–0–415–23354–5
Pb: 978–0–415–23355–2

Available at all good bookshops
For ordering and further information please visit:
www.routledge.com

Related titles from Routledge

Neolithic

Susan McCarter

How did people move from caves to condos? When did the rich become different from everyone else? Who built Stonehenge? Who invented the plough?

The answer to all these questions lies in the Neolithic era, during which people's lives were irrevocably altered by the invention of agriculture.

This book is a lively and engaging introduction to a momentous period, one during which our ancestors stopped hunting and gathering and built permanent, settled villages where they could develop farming, herding and new technologies: in short where they laid the foundations for the patterns of modern life.

After familiarising the reader with essential archaeological and genetic terms and concepts, McCarter condenses the latest evidence from scientific analyses as varied as deep-sea coring, pollen identification, radiometric dating and DNA research into an up-to-date account which despite the use of complex material remains accessible to even the novice reader.

Focusing primarily on sites in southwest Asia, Neolithic addresses questions such as:

- Which plants and animals were the first to be domesticated, and how?
- How did life change when people began farming?
- What were the first villages like?
- What do we know about the social, political and religious life of these early societies?
- How did the Neolithic Revolution affect human health?

Lavishly illustrated with almost a hundred images, this enjoyable book is an ideal introduction both for students of archaeology and for general readers interested in our past.

Hb: 978–0–415–36413–3
Pb: 978–0–415–36414–0

Available at all good bookshops
For ordering and further information please visit:
www.routledge.com